THE VIRGIN DIARIES

Compiled and edited by
Kimberley A. Johnson
and
Ann Werner

Design and formatting
by Ralph Faust

Published in the United States by ARK Stories in cooperation with Createspace.com

Cover Design by Ralph Faust

This book is dedicated to virgins everywhere.

We would like to thank those who were helpful in getting this book completed. First and foremost, a big thank you to all the people who participated in this project. Without you, there would be no book. To Laura Stroube Hughes for her suggestions. We took them! To Cheryl Sanfilippo for her unbridled enthusiasm. Oh that everyone could be like you and thanks for helping us come up with the title.

Contents

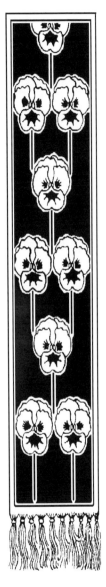

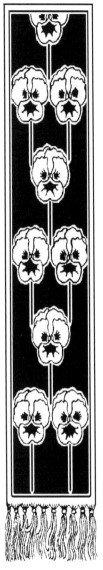

?¿?¿?¿?¿?¿ A Note to Parents

When I have asked parents of children thirteen years old or younger if they would let them read this book, I was usually met with a conservative attitude. They would look noticeably uncomfortable and say something like "Well, maybe when they are fifteen or older."

It is not my place to advise anyone on how to parent but I will share with you how it was for me.

I was a very shy girl when it came to sex. I didn't want to talk about it and it pretty much grossed me out. I remember asking my mother at around the age of six what sex was. In a very matter of fact way, she explained that it was when a man puts his penis into a woman's vagina. I was HORRIFIED at the idea. As horrified as I was, I do remember asking her that question more than once and she always told me the same thing.

The summer I turned nine, I started watching a soap opera because as I was changing channels, looking for something to watch, I happened upon a scene where a teenaged boy and girl were having first time sex. I cannot tell you how riveted I was by this. I would never have admitted this to anyone, especially my parents.

The same year, a few months into the fourth grade, a girlfriend of mine showed me and a few others the book *Forever* by Judy Blume; a book about first time sex. We all sat at recess reading only the sex parts. That same day after school I ran to the closest bookstore and purchased it. It had over two hundred pages. It was the first "real" book I'd ever read and I was finished the following day. I must have read that book ten times if I read it once.

The point to this is that no matter how young or shy your child is, the fact is they ARE interested in sex. They want to know as much as they can, even if they think it's gross and have no intention of having it.

Children usually do not want to talk explicitly with their parents about it. That's not even an age thing. Do you, at this point in your life, want to speak to either one of your parents explicitly about sex? I don't and I'm 41.

As much as you want your child to abstain and as much as you wish to shield them from sex, it's on their minds. They are curious creatures and if left alone with literature or movies on the subject, they will read or watch.

When I came up with the idea of putting this book together, I wanted to make it for virgins. I wanted to give them the tools to make an informed decision when the time is right. I hope this book offers that. Nothing is sugar coated. These are real people telling their experiences. I can honestly say with 100% certainty, if this was available when I was a virgin, I would have read it and I believe that perhaps it would have colored my choice in a positive way on why and how I lost my virginity.

Kimberley A. Johnson
January 2010

?¿?¿?¿?¿?¿ **Introduction**

When's the last time you sat down with your grandmother or grandfather and talked about sex? Let's face it. Every virgin wants to know about sex. But nobody really wants to talk about it. Parents are often embarrassed when their kids ask about it. Some even object to the subject being taught in schools. It's a strange thing in our culture. We rail against it, yet it's all around us. We sell everything from deodorant to cars utilizing sex and it's all over television and in the movies. We see bare butts, breasts and more. Female teen idols dress like hookers and gyrate in a mimic of the sexual act and yet the whole country goes into an uproar when Janet Jackson's middle-aged breast flops out during the Super Bowl. It's a fair assessment to say we are a society conflicted when it comes to the subject of sex.

Conflicted or not, the fact is once we get to a certain age, our hormones kick into high gear, peer pressure comes to bear and sex, whether it's having it, thinking about having it, wondering what it's like or hearing about it from our friends, becomes an almost overwhelming priority.

Where to go? What to do? Ask your parents? Maybe a fractional part of the population can do that. A tiny fractional part. Enlist the aid of a priest, a nun or a minister? It's safe to say that most likely the only advice there would be "Don't do it" and any other questions would be rendered moot. In school, perhaps some answers concerning the biology of it might be addressed, depending on where you are and the social forces exerted on that school district. But the questions people have about sex: What's it like? How did it feel? Were there regrets? If you had it to do over again, would you? Can you give me any advice? These are the questions that won't get answered in a sex education or biology class.

They are the questions we set out to answer in this book. On these pages you will find seventy-two stories from people who range in age from twenty to seventy-seven. There are thirty-six stories from women and thirty-six from men. We know some of these people but most are people who answered our call for volunteers on the Internet. All of them are anonymous.

Being anonymous frees you to say what really happened, how you really felt, what it really meant. And if you aren't exactly the poster child for safe sex, for great sex or grand passion, nobody knows. Your story stands by itself. Anonymity made it possible for us to gather this great collection from people of all ages, male and female, gay and straight, from every part of the country.

Sex is something we all share in common. We all have our own ideas of how it should or shouldn't be. As diverse as these people are, a lot of common threads emerged throughout the accounts told on these pages. We think that's a good thing, a wonderful thing, because it serves to remind us that we are all looking for the same things, no matter who we are, where we are from or what our sexual preferences are. We are all human beings and we share, or suppress, common emotions.

For young people who have that burning question, here is a wealth of experience. For the rest of us, these stories are entertaining and sure to strike a chord somewhere along the way. Some are funny, some are touching, some are a little bit sad and some could be categorized as cautionary tales but they are all real and that's what's important.

There are stories included that don't address all the questions posed on the questionnaire we compiled. We kept them because they were still interesting, if not complete. No matter who you are, we think you'll find a bit of yourself in these accounts related by the wonderful people who decided to share one of life's most pivotal experiences.

We did our best to stay true to what was originally said or written but did minor editing, like correcting spelling and punctuation in places to make reading the stories easier. We also removed overly explicit sexual language, although you will find the f-word in a few places. We also changed the names and locations because we were afraid someone didn't follow instructions and we didn't want anyone's identity revealed.

A couple of the women we approached declined to tell their stories because they had been molested. We can only imagine the pain suffered by victims of sexual assault and/or molestation and we respect the feelings of those who chose not to share their first consensual experience. Each of us has our demons and it was never our intention to stir up bad or painful memories. There is, however, one story where it is mentioned that the first consensual experience was colored by the fact that molestation had taken place sometime earlier. It wasn't expanded upon and we didn't ask for more than was given. There is also another entry that mentions the date rape of a friend and how that impacted the author's perceptions, as well as that of her friends.

It is important to note that this was done informally. Neither one of us is a psychologist, a psychiatrist or a scientist. Because we don't want the reader to view the accounts through the prism of our perception, we have declined to comment on any of the stories, with one exception. That one has a footnote and the reason for it is self-evident. To the best of our knowledge all of the stories are from people in the United States. When posting on the Internet, we concentrated on the larger U.S. cities because websites get more hits in these areas. When posting in smaller cities, we rarely got a response.

Initially we set out to interview only women. Later on we realized men's stories were needed to give a broader perspective. One of the women who responded to our Internet ad was gay and that prompted us to seek out more accounts from gay people.

We consider ourselves quite lucky to have received some wonderful, well-written responses to our call for answers. To all of the men and women who got the guidelines, followed instructions and shared your first experience, we salute you!

The Questions

We supplied a short set of guidelines and had three questionnaires. They were all nearly the same, with only minor variations that were specific to gender and/or sexual orientation. The following is the template we used. The only differences were that we substituted she or her instead of he or him when we sent them to men and substituted he/she and him/her when sending them to gay respondents. The additional questions for our gay respondents are in italics.

Guidelines:

All stories will be in essay format. You can make an essay or one will be made from the answers you provide. If you do not wish to write an essay, cut and paste the questions (below) in an email and answer each one with as much detail as possible. PLEASE refrain from short answers like yes or no. We cannot make that into an essay and don't want to waste your time. TO BE CLEAR, we are looking for the whole story, how you felt before, during and after; your fears, your pride, etc. If you arrange your own essay, please answer EACH question. Also remember to CHANGE your and any names and any place that might identify you or someone else.

If you lost your virginity with both sexes, you may, if you wish, include both stories. We are more interested in consensual stories, no rape or molestation. If you were molested, you may, if you wish, discuss what impact it had. The audience for this will be young people. We are NOT interested in sexually explicit language and will not use it.

- How old are you now?

- How old were you?

- Had you any expectation of what it would be like or how you wanted it to be?

- Who was he? How did you know him? How old was he?

- *At what age did you realize you are gay? If your first experience was with a member of the opposite sex, how did your being gay have an impact?*

- How long had you known him before losing your virginity with him?

⁇ What kind of advice did your parents give you?

⁇ What kinds of advice or rumors did you hear about sex from your friends when you were a virgin?

⁇ Did you get advice from a religious figure(s)...what was it?

⁇ Where did you do it?

⁇ Did you know it would happen? Did it take you by surprise?

⁇ Did you use birth control? If so what kind?

⁇ In detail what was it like for you? What was going through your mind? Did it hurt?

⁇ Were you happy? Sad? Scared?

⁇ Was he respectful of you while it was happening? Was he gentle...awkward...sweet?

⁇ Did he have trouble getting it in? (*if there was penetration involved*)

⁇ What was the best part? What was the worst part?

⁇ How did you feel about yourself afterward? Regret? Pride?

⁇ How did you feel about him?

⁇ Did you tell anyone afterward?

⁇ What happened with/to him? Do you still know him?

⁇ Why did you choose to lose your virginity at that time with that person?

⁇ Did that experience color your attitudes toward sex...if so, how and for how long?

⁇ Now that you are older, how do you feel when you look back on the experience?

⁇ If you had it to do all over again, would you change any part of it? How and why?

⁇ What advice would you give to virgins?

⁇ Is there anything else you would like to add?

*T*he good part, though, was that I learned almost everything about sex in those few minutes, especially what not to do.

Male: I am 44. I was 13.

Raquel Welch had always been my favorite actress but in the last year she had a different effect on me. Whenever I saw her on television or in a movie, I got an immediate erection. Even a picture in *T.V. Guide* would do it. So tall and curvy and dark-haired. I dreamed of meeting someone like her and then I saw Shelly. She lived the next street over and we ran into each other going to school one day. She was 5'7", a curvy brunette with the biggest breasts I had ever seen on a junior high girl. She was just like Raquel to me.

On average, adult men think about sex every seven seconds.
- Kanner, Bernice. 2005. Are You Normal About Sex, Love, and Relationships?
La Vergne, TN: Lightning Source, Inc.
Source: www.randomhistory.com

I had no idea what to do, what to expect, or even what sex was. But I knew I wanted to find out. My parents were no help. They were immigrants and the very idea of discussing sex with anyone, including each other, was abhorrent. I inherited this guilt and was too embarrassed to ask them or my friends about it. My friend Frank, however, told me that he saw his parents doing it and I should hug her tight and scream in her ear and she will scream back.

After a month, I finally got the nerve to ask her on a date. I had seen Burt Reynolds ask Raquel to dinner and take her to a romantic Italian restaurant. Shelly didn't seem to mind that I was 5'2" and I think she liked me too, so she said yes. I took her to Pizza Hut, which was as close as I could come in my little town. We had fun and on the way home we passed some small woods and she stopped. She leaned down and kissed me and asked if I wanted to make out in the woods. This was definitely a surprise. It turns out she was far more experienced than me and just came out and asked me if I wanted to see her naked. I don't remember actually being able to form the word yes but I think she took my awkward shifting and mumbling for yes and it happened right there on our coats.

The only thing on my mind, besides sheer joy from seeing my beautiful nude Shelly, was just keep your cool and try not to act like a virgin. That plan crumbled quickly. I was all over her but nowhere in particular. She stopped me and looked in my eyes and said, "You ever do this before?" I said, "Yes!" She laughed and put my hands where she wanted them, until

I figured out what to do. I touched her gently, even carefully. I didn't want to hurt her, though she outweighed me by twenty pounds. I was so happy. When she touched me and put it inside herself, I truly felt blissful. She was wet and not exactly a virgin, so I had no trouble entering her. Then I instinctively began moving and that was it. It was over. I was confused, she was disappointed and our romance ended right there. That was the worst part, that she wouldn't go out with me again.

The good part, though, was that I learned almost everything about sex in those few minutes, especially what not to do. In spite of it, I was grateful to her and felt like a man. I also knew that I had to learn to control myself, to prolong the blissful feelings as long as I could. Then she would enjoy it too—and maybe want to do it again. This informed my attitude toward sex in a positive way. It compelled me to learn more about women, not only sexually but I explored my fascination with them. I still don't know anything but at least I keep trying.

She moved away the next summer and I never saw her again. For a long time, I thought if I ever saw her again, I would feel embarrassed and ashamed and have to apologize. But now, at forty-four, I smile at the thought of it and in writing this I can laugh, because I knew no better and treated her as well as I could. My actions were foolish but I was sincere.

That is the advice I would give a virgin. Be sincere and honest with your partner. If they aren't understanding, they are not the one for your first time. If they listen to you, smile and treat you with love, you will re-member this moment as beautiful and will feel bliss.

*T**he only rumor I heard was that if you thought you might be pregnant you could shake up a bottle of [1]cola and insert it and that might abort a baby.***

Female: I am 77 now. I was 15 years old.

I had no expectations growing up, we didn't calculate it the way we do today. It just happened. He was my love for three years, he was also fifteen. We were going to get married but he became ill and his mother didn't want us to get married—it was a whole big thing.

Advice from parents? Are you kidding? You must be kidding. Those were the days when you had to sneak around and you didn't let your girlfriends know and then you found out later that they were doing the same thing with their boyfriends and it was always with a boyfriend. Not just indiscriminately sleeping around the way they do today. The two of us—it just came naturally, we learned together.

I didn't discuss it with my friends. I knew more than anybody, always; not because I'd been experienced but because I had an open dialogue with my mother. I wasn't living with her but I could talk with her about anything. I knew what was going on in the world. The only rumor I heard was that if you thought you might be pregnant you could shake up a bottle of [1]cola and it insert it and that might abort a baby. Or start an abortion.

It took place in my home. It wasn't like today when you watch movies and they say "tonight's the night." I mean that's so calculated. We cared for one another, we were young and that was it. We used a condom. Those were the things that you couldn't go in the store and buy. He got the condoms. I didn't ask him how.

[1] The brand name of the soft drink mentioned in the original story sent to us has been changed to the generic term.

It was very natural. It was very nice. I wanted to do it again. Afterward, I felt very nice, we snuggled, you know. I felt very happy, very content, just very close. We were both children of divorce so it gave us both kind of an anchor.

I didn't tell anyone about it afterward.

I still know him.

I always liked sex, depending on who my partner was.

Looking back, it was very sweet and a very important part of my life because I had somebody to hold, to be with. I was relatively insecure in myself. It just made me feel close to somebody and that I needed to be a part of somebody's life. That's what it did. We had boyfriends then, we didn't have parties where people switched partners and it was just different. You went steady and eventually you had sex. You loved each other, whether it was real love or not. It was something you did to be close.

My advice to virgins would be first of all, know what you're doing. Be of an age, at least fifteen or sixteen and be sure that you really care for the boy and you don't want to just experiment with the act.

Vanessa was basically a maid... She was like Lisa Bonet

Male: I'm 40 years old. I was 15 years old when it happened.

The only expectations I had were from what I had seen in movies and from what friends had told me. I had little experience with girls and hooking up but I knew I was crazy about girls. To be honest, my parents didn't give me any advice when it came to sex or even losing my virginity. My dad talked to me about sex on a fishing trip when I was about ten years old. It was the basic info. That was it. I didn't get any advice from religious figures. I only remember hearing a woman's vagina was so soft, so incredible feeling. I never heard any advice. A lot of my friends had not had sex either at that time so advice was pretty non-existent. All I knew is that I really wanted to have sex. I loved women. I loved the beauty of women. I loved getting attention from girls. I was amazed with the female body and I wanted to explore the female body in a bad way. Every inch.

My mother hired a woman to clean the house in the summer of 1984. Vanessa was basically a maid: a twenty-three year old, light skinned black woman. Her skin was like coffee with cream. She was like Lisa Bonet, a beautiful face and her body was just beautiful. When I first met her I thought I picked up some weird vibe—you know, her looking at me in an odd way, smiling at me etc. I just figured I was looking for a sign that she may have liked me. My mom left with Vanessa to drop her off at the metro and when she came back she said Vanessa was talking about how cute she thought I was. Needless to say, it made my day.

Vanessa returned two weeks later to clean the house again. My high school summer vacation had started a week prior. The situation was pretty unique too. Both of my parents worked, so they were not home. My sister was away, so it was just me and a buddy who had crashed the night before. My mom told me in the morning that Vanessa would be at the house all day cleaning and asked that my buddy and me stay out of her way and not to give her any trouble.

Vanessa was upstairs cleaning the bedrooms when I heard

her call me into my parents' room to talk. I told my buddy I would be right back and off I went. When I went into the bedroom, she came out of the master bath and asked me to sit down. I sat on the end of my parents' bed and she kneeled in front of me. She looked up at me and said she needed to tell me some things. I said, "Sure, what's up?" She started to tell me how she hadn't been able to stop thinking about me and that she was really attracted to me. I told her that I thought she was very pretty (I truly had no clue what to say at this point but had a feeling something was about to go down) and had thought about her as well. It was then she looked at me and said she liked me a lot. I asked her how much she liked me and well, her response I can still hear in my head to this day. She looked right at me and said, "I like you enough to fuck your brains out." My response was "wow!" She then asked for my hand and placed it over her heart, which was slightly above one of her breasts underneath her thin yellow t-shirt (sic). She told me to feel her heart beating and it really was beating quite a bit. She then moved my hand over one of her breasts and squeezed. She was not wearing a bra. It was at that point she stood up, pushed me back on the bed and started kissing my face and neck. She breathed into my ear "get your friend out of here". Then she got up off of me, smiled at me lying on the bed and asked "ok?" And I responded with an "ok" and bolted out of the room.

I truly had zero idea it would happen and was pretty much blown away. We didn't use any birth control at all. I didn't even think about protection/birth control to be honest. I did know enough to pull out at the point of no return the few times we had sex that day.

It was an amazing experience. I mean, it was obviously unlike anything I had ever gone through before. I remember so clearly it's scary. I told my buddy he had to get out because I had to do something for my parents. I ran back upstairs and Vanessa was in the master bathroom with a bottle of Mr. Clean in one hand and a rag in her other hand. I told her my friend was gone and the door was locked. She threw the rag and Mr. Clean on the floor and pushed me back on the bed.

It was amazing. I started kissing her as she lay on the bed. She then took off her tiny t-shirt and I just continued kissing her. I literally devoured every beautiful inch of her body. She took my shirt off and proceeded to kiss my chest, my neck—it was incredible. Soon after, she slid out of her shorts to reveal the rest of her slender, toned body. I remember specifically kissing down her legs to her pedicured toes and coming slowly back up the inside of her legs to get to that special place I had been wanting to go. It was then she stopped me and said we should move to the floor because she just got done putting the clean sheets on my parents' bed. I didn't argue.

She grabbed my hand, smiled at me and led me to the floor at the foot of the bed. She was on her back and I was on my knees just looking at her and she then started tugging at my shorts. I helped her take them off and once they were off she started stroking me and I bent down to continue kissing her body everywhere and anywhere.

I lasted just under two minutes that first time. I remember telling Vanessa I was going to cum and there was just no way I could stop it. I pulled out of her and placed my hand on me but she quickly replaced my hand with her hand and she finished me on her stomach. She was telling me how nice I felt, how beautiful she thought I was and I was just looking down at her, unable to speak, thinking how incredible this woman was and how beautiful she was. It was an unbelievable moment I shall never forget. I collapsed on her body and then the phone started ringing. I got up, went to my mom's nightstand to answer it and would you believe it was my mother on the other end? I was flushed and out of breath but managed to hold a conversation as best I could. I watched Vanessa gather her clothes off the floor, off the bed and walk towards the bedroom door. She looked back at me as I was on the phone and she smiled and mouthed "thank you" before leaving the room. It was only 11am. My mom in the meantime was asking me how Vanessa was doing at the house and if she was doing her job or just screwing around. I mean seriously—what are the odds?

I was very respectful during and afterwards. Matter of fact, I wanted to make sure she felt as good as she could possibly feel. I literally kissed every inch of her body and kept asking if that felt good or if this felt good. It was important for me to make her feel good and the funny thing is that this is something I carried with me throughout my life. I am a giver when it comes to sex. I love to make the person I am with feel as good as possible and will do whatever they wish. I was definitely awkward though. There were a couple times I just wasn't sure what to do but Vanessa was so sweet. She guided me when I looked like I was lost but I was always very gentle.

Her reaction was more centered on determination and the fact that we were going to have sex. It was odd. She told me later in the day that if I hadn't cooperated with her she would have raped me. She said that with a bit of a smile. I laughed and said "yeah right" and she looked right at me and said she was very serious. Her reaction during our lovemaking the first time it happened was very passionate.

The best part for me was the foreplay. I felt odd afterwards but felt great at the same time. I regretted it somewhat though. The reason? I had met a girl earlier that spring who lived down the street with her aunt. This girl was up from Florida and was taking ballet at the local School of Ballet. It was a spring love kind of thing and would you believe I felt guilty for having sex with my maid because of another girl? At the same time, I recognized the fact that what had happened to me was something that was pretty unique. I mean, I was living a *Penthouse* letter right there in my own house, during summer vacation and I wasn't even a sophomore in high school yet. Later in the afternoon I had a talk with her explaining how I felt and that there was this girl who I had met and Vanessa asked if I regretted what happened. I told her no, I didn't regret it but wasn't sure how I was feeling. She was cool about it.

I thought she was nice and thought she was very pretty but there was something about her determination and the fact that she told me she would have raped me if I didn't cooperate. She also went on to tell me she was going to teach me a lot of things. She was going to make me the best lover she could. She was already planning on screwing me throughout the summer. Any time she was at the house cleaning, it would be best for me to plan on "getting fucked" as she put it—and all over the house: kitchen, laundry room, living room, my room (which happened later that day).

Afterwards, I called my buddy who had spent the night. She was down in the kitchen when I made the call so I was trying to be extra quiet. My buddy and his brother were on the phone and Bill asked, "What the hell happened earlier?" I replied with "Dude, I just fucked the maid." Neither of them believed it—I mean who would? I explained a little of the story and then heard Vanessa coming upstairs so I hung up. The story of the maid and me actually became a favorite story in the hallways of the all boy high school I attended. By the time I was a junior, the entire class was pretty aware of it.

To make a long story short, I told my mom Vanessa didn't do much and essentially worked it so that my mom fired her. I was too freaked out by everything. I started getting worried she was going to get pregnant or that I had an STD—I mean my brain went into overdrive.

It happened so fast and was so surreal that I literally felt as if I had no choice. Plus, I recognized it was a unique situation for a 15-year-old kid and I just rolled with it. It was amazing. If anything, I wanted more of it and wanted a lot of it. Unfortunately though, more sex would not happen for me until the following summer at the beach.

My attitude towards sex was centered more on the "giving" nature of it. I was really taken with making Vanessa feel as good as I could. I loved seeing her reactions and loved hearing her catch her breath when I touched her. To this day, I am not satisfied unless my partner is satisfied.

I think it was the coolest, wildest experience and would not have traded it for anything. I ended up having a handful of sexual experiences with Vanessa that day. All in all it really was a wild day. The first family member to get home was my mom and that was at 5:30pm. Needless to say, from 11am to 5:30pm there were not a lot of clothes on.

If I had it to do all over again, I probably would not have pushed my mom to fire her. I felt bad about that to be honest. And I would have been having sex all summer!!!

The only advice I would give is to go with your gut. Don't feel pressured and be sure you truly want it to happen.

I kept thinking when is this going to feel good?

Female: I am 35. I was 15.

My expectations were that it would be romantic and sensational. His name was Wally and he was a local friend of a friend. He was eighteen. I knew him about eight months before losing my virginity with him.

The advice I got from my parents was that if you have sex, you get pregnant.

> *"It is an infantile superstition of the human spirit that virginity would be thought a virtue and not the barrier that separates ignorance from knowledge."*
>
> *- Voltaire*
> *Source: www.quotesdaddy.com*

I had only had one friend who was not a virgin at the time and she made it sound like it was fun and exciting—why wait if you have someone who cares for you and also this will cure the curiosity.

I didn't get any advice from religious figures.

We did it in a vacant home that his mother owned and that he was remodeling at the time. I knew it would happen. We had talked about it several times and had it planned for this particular evening.

We used a condom.

It hurt very badly. It didn't help that my first time would be with a man who had more than average girth and length. I was scared to death. I kept thinking when is this going to feel good? It never did—not even over the course of trying for several months. I had on white pants and when I got home I had blood everywhere. It looked like I had started my period and I was horrified.

He was respectful. He knew I was scared. He was not a virgin. It was awkward as I was not one hundred percent comfortable with my body—especially to have a man look at it in the nude for the very first time. He was very gentle and tried to make the best of the situation. He definitely had trouble getting his penis inside of me. I was very tight.

There was no best part for me. The blood, emotion and pain were the worst part.

I didn't feel great about myself afterward. I was confused and I feel as though I should have waited—not that he wasn't the right one but I was too young.

I did care for him. He was my first true boyfriend and it was so fantastic to have someone who cared about me. I think I was more in love with the novelty of having a boyfriend.

I told my girlfriend who introduced us.

Last I heard he moved to another state with his wife. I have not seen or spoken to him in over thirteen years.

I chose to lose my virginity with him because it was my first chance to try it.

I was afraid to do it again. I did not want to experience the pain. It was at least two years before I can honestly say I truly enjoyed sex for myself.

I don't have any real regret. I'm a very curious person. He was a nice guy and things could have been a lot worse. I wish I had been a bit older and more mature for my first time. The part I would change, if I could, would be that I probably would have waited longer and tried more foreplay with my mate. All for maturity reasons and pleasure for me, not just my mate.

Don't rush, you have a lifetime ahead of you! Make it fun, make it with someone who really loves you and you really love. A person who has marriage potential for you. If you are not willing to take on a child, you should not be having intercourse with anyone. Intercourse is a huge risk and it should not be taken lightly. Curiosity could ruin your life.

*I*t just pains me to know that I may have let the love of my life get away, all because we were too young to be too serious.

Male: I am now 23 but at the time I lost my virginity I was 17. We both were.

She was my girlfriend and we had been dating each other long distance for about a year and a half at that point. We met when we both worked in a restaurant together. We were very young, in love and stupid but I repeat myself.

I didn't know what to expect. My Italian Catholic parents weren't going to give any tips (except be safe), neither were the priests. I just figured it would be good and that I wanted to do it. My friends were no help, as I was the first one to have sex. Some advice was to use lubrication. Other than that, not much advice was given.

I don't know why it happened when it did. We didn't plan on it, though I just had a feeling it would happen that day. I just had a hunch that we were headed that way. So I made sure to bring the condoms that were at the ready for about a year.

We had been helping her friend set up her new apartment. We used to go there to hang out alone. We knew she was going to be at work for hours. The funny thing was that we didn't want to do it on her bed but there was an extra mattress on the floor. It was without any sheets, so we laid a towel down. The evening news was on in the background. We were a bit paranoid, so we used a condom and the spermicidal foam, which is unromantic to say the least. The first time putting on the condom was, I think, the funniest and most awkward part but after that it all went smoothly.

I was very anxious beforehand because I really didn't know what it would be like. That was the worst part. I also didn't want to come too quickly. It didn't hurt me but it hurt her a little but as she put it "a good hurt." I was happy/relieved/contented at the end. I would like to think I was respectful. This was my girlfriend for a long time, so it was all these things: It was awkward and gentle and I think it was sweet. I would consider it making love and not having sex. The best part, and the thing I will always remember, was her eyes. She had these really pretty blue eyes and the first time I went inside her, her pupils got really wide. It did that several more times when we did it again later but I'll always remember looking into her eyes and seeing that. Afterwards, I felt more of a completeness and a bond between us. I was then and still am in love with her. It was the right time and the right person. Sometimes you just know.

I told whoever would listen, as long as they were under thirty and not related to me but it was a slow burn at first, didn't want to rush the secret.

I don't know where she is now. We lost touch about a year ago after dating for four and a half years. After we broke up, I could not have sex with someone unless I was dating them or felt deeply about them. I don't think I would have felt that way if I had not been with her and had I not been totally in love. I think that attitude still sticks with me, at least a little.

Now that I am older, I look back on that first time and it's a bittersweet feeling. It was very nice and I really enjoyed it but now, I think I miss that girl so much. I've been in love again but I don't think it's the same. I share a bond with her that no one else can ever have. I wouldn't change a moment.

My advice to virgins would be not to rush into it with the first person that comes along, take your time, care about that person. You'll remember it much happier than if you were just drunk and horny at some party. Writing all this makes me sad. I am at a crossroads in my life women-wise and it just pains me to know that I may have let the love of my life get away, all because we were too young to be too serious.

I was primarily focused on having it be "perfect" like it seemed to be on television.

Female: I am 36 years old now. I was 23, I think.

I always thought it would be the most romantic thing in the world. Never did it cross my mind that it would hurt. The people that made love in the soap operas always looked so relaxed and beautiful when they did it. I wanted it to be just like that for me. I wanted my hair to fall just right, not a smudge on my make-up. I wanted to look my best at all times, no sweating and I was primarily focused on having it be perfect like it seemed to be on television. Also, I knew that when I did it, my mother expected me to get married afterwards, so I felt tremendously pressured to be sure that it was the best I'd ever had. Since I had no one else to compare it to, there was no room for misconceptions on my part. But I figured, if I was wrong, there would be plenty of time to iron it all out after we got married.

Bill was his name. He was 25 years old (an older man!) I met him in community theater. We were in *Bullshot Crummond*, a dinner theater comedy. He was Bullshot and I was Rosemary Fenton (his damsel in distress). I guess I remained his damsel in distress even after the play. He had stolen my heart forever. I was shy and afraid to be touched. I guess I knew Bill for at least six months before asking my mother permission to sleep with him.

My mother and I spoke about the forbidden topic of love making before I ventured out. She told me about condoms and diaphragms and wanted to know which one I preferred. Since I was so naïve, I didn't know what either one was, so she suggested condoms. She told me that love making was only to happen between two people who loved each other and who had a commitment to one another, like a man and his wife. But, if we were going to be married and if I was SURE that he was going to ask me to marry him someday, then it would be okay but we were not to tell my father anything about it. My dad wasn't supportive of the idea.

My friends weren't having sex that I know of. I remember a girl who had sex in high school but everyone talked negatively about her. Everyone said she was a slut. Actually, everyone that had sex was a slut. Sex was a no-no. It was okay if you had sex but you just had to hide it. As long as you didn't tell anyone about it, it was fine. The real problem was if someone had sex they could never keep it a secret, so only a select few people were told but eventually everyone in the world was sworn to secrecy. So, with that said, everyone walked around with a wealth of information regarding someone else's "hot night last night" but no one ever said anything about it.

> *Confidence is the sexiest thing a woman can have.*
> *It's much sexier than any body part.*
> *- Aimee Mullins, Oprah Magazine, May 2004*
> *Source: www.quotationspage.com*

I never had advice from any religious figures. When I finally decided it was time, my mom suggested we make love at our house in my room. That way if anything were to go wrong she would be down the hall and around the corner at the other end of the house. We had to plan it when my father was gone, though. My dad used to take weekends once in a while to "have his space" from us. I later learned he had quite a few affairs but I didn't know it then. Mom was so good about keeping it hidden. So Dad went away for the weekend and Bill came over. We played cards and watched TV with my mom, then she confidently said, "Well, good night. See you two in the morning. I'll make breakfast for you."

Bill and I went to bed and I was very nervous. He knew I had been molested in my life, so he took things very slow and was careful to explain why he was suggesting positions, or foreplay. He was quite a prince, he knew what he was doing. He didn't have trouble taking control of the situation. He was not a virgin. He was very sensitive too. I cried a little bit when he finally got himself comfortable inside me and he cried too, asking me if I wanted him to stop. I asked him "We're doing it, right? You're in and we're doing it, right?" He replied "Yes, I am." So I said, "Then don't stop." We used a condom and it hurt a lot. I didn't have an orgasm the first time. Not at all. I pretended I did though. I moaned and made sure my hair fell just right and was careful not to mess up my make-up. I was always aware of positioning my body to reflect my sexiest pose and was careful to always have my most flattering side profile facing him. He seemed to be pleased. He was very surprised to hear I had an orgasm. I don't think he believed me either. Oh well, I made it the way I thought it should be. My favorite part was cuddling afterwards in his arms.

It was so wonderful after he was finally done. Then I excused myself to go to the bathroom and fix my hair and face. I came back to the room—a vision. I felt like a woman. Finally felt like a woman. Bill loved me. He was the first man in my life who truly loved me and wanted to take care of me. I never wanted that feeling to ever end. We were in a fairy tale. I felt as if this were the beginning of a new life for myself. He would take care of me forever and I would always be his. Nothing could stop us.

The next morning, I told my Mom how it was after he went home. She was very happy for me and was so happy that I was happy. She explained to me that we would have to tell my father but she wouldn't tell him that it happened in the house. I agreed. I knew my father would be happy for me when he found out how much I loved Bill and that I planned to marry him.

When my mother told my father what happened he wasn't happy. As a matter of fact, he was so angry I thought he would kill me. He did kill me emotionally. Two days after he got home from his affair, I was out to a movie with Bill. He had just dropped me off at home and I walked into the house. The sliding glass doors were open: It was dark and there were dead leaves that had blown in and were scattered all over the carpet. The place was silent, except for the wind. It was very cold. My brother's door was shut as was my parents'. I walked into my room and turned on the light. There, neatly stacked in the middle of my bedroom floor, was a pile of my baby pictures, adolescent pictures and family photos that I was in. All were ripped up into tiny little pieces only revealing portions of my face so I could tell what the pictures were of. Beside the pile was a note from my father full of hateful comments and awful insults including name calling and dehumanizing vocabulary. Signed "Love, Dad." That was the end of my relationship with my father. I learned to live with it but I never got over it. It destroyed my life.

Bill was nothing like my father. Bill was safe. He was sincere and sensitive; he took care of me. He always wanted to know what would make me happy and he was patient. But most importantly, Bill listened to me.

On a sad note, Bill had a drinking problem and had been dealing drugs. I didn't know this. I was too naïve to pick up on it at the time. My mother and father inevitably made me stop seeing him and I was devastated. Bill's mother sent him away to a drug rehab center and I was not to see him again. I was so sad. I thought about killing myself. I hated my father. I hated every man on earth except Bill. He was the only good thing in my life and I wasn't good enough to have or deserve any happiness. This was the toughest time of my life. After a year I got over him but never forgot him. I saw him about three years later and we had both changed. We talked for a while over a cup of coffee and sat in amazement (sic) at how much we had grown up and solved the world's problems. We shook hands afterwards and said good-bye. That was the last time I saw him.

So much has changed since then. I'll always think good thoughts when I think of Bill. I didn't think I'd ever meet anyone so wonderful but I did. I met my husband ten years later. Love making is special to me because I deserve to be loved in the best way possible. If I had to do it again, I wouldn't change a thing. Although I've had some really rough times in my life, I feel like each experience has had a direct effect on who I have become. I am so happy to be who I am today. I don't think I would love myself to the deep degree that I do if anything had been different. I look forward to love making all the time and am excited about having a family of my own since I am confident I will be a fantastic mother and my husband will be the best father. This I know.

When my daughter is grown and ready to give away her virginity, I will be a good listener. I will be happy for her and accepting of her choice. I will direct her to safety and go over all birth control options and will take her out to lunch after going to the Planned Parenthood center, etc. My husband and I both plan to be very close to our children and supportive of their personal feelings and needs. Our goal is to make it as comfortable as possible and to be supportive and understanding to our children and friends who wish to express their love to each other through making love.

I was also nervous, because my parents were home and just down the hallway.

Male: I am 22. I was 15.

I didn't really have much expectation. I wasn't expecting it to happen when it did. So I didn't get to premeditate on it much. She was my girlfriend at the time. Age fifteen as well. I'd known her about seven or eight months. We were together for about two or three when it first happened.

I had no advice from parents. None. They didn't really know. When they first found out I was sexually active, the only real advice they gave me was to use protection. Not much advice from friends either. None of my friends at the time were sexually active. No advice from any religious figures.

We did it in my bedroom at home. It took me by surprise for sure. She had already had one experience before me, so she probably had an idea it was going to happen. We didn't use birth control.

It felt amazing, of course. Something I had never known of. Because at that time, I had never even masturbated before. I wasn't big on sex really. I liked girls. But I was oblivious to the "world of sex." I had NO idea how it felt at all. I was also nervous, because my parents were home and just down the hallway. And at the same time, it was a beautiful thing because I also cared for my girlfriend very much at the time. I was respectful—a little awkward, it being my first time and all. I even made sure that she wanted to go through with it. I didn't want her making a decision she might regret.

She wasn't exactly ecstatic. But I'm sure she enjoyed it. She took more charge than I did.

Did I have trouble entering her? Ha, yeah. Not too long though. She kind of directed me.

The best part was the actual physical feeling of it while it was happening. I mean I had never felt like that EVER. So, you can only imagine. I had goose bumps! The worst part was that the girl I was with had some sort of stench. A stinky stench, which to this day, I still don't really understand.

The average male produces several million new sperm daily. Conversely, a female is born with a finite amount of eggs and will produce no more than that throughout her lifetime.

- Keesling, Barbara. 2000. *Rx Sex: Making Love Is the Best Medicine.* Alameda, CA: Hunter House, Inc.
Source: www.randomhistory.com

I'm assuming it came from her private area but I never asked her.

Afterward, I felt like a grown up. It changed our relationship in a huge way. We were sooo comfortable with each other after that. I felt so strongly about her after. My jealousy became stronger. I don't really know how to explain it. I guess I became so much more attached.

I told all my friends.

We eventually, after about ten months total, broke up. We both moved on and stayed somewhat friends. She ended up moving on before I did and wound up getting pregnant by her next boyfriend. Years have gone by, we still keep in touch. In fact, I spoke to her just a few days ago. I still consider her a good friend of mine.

I didn't choose it. It chose me.

Yes, that experience did color my attitudes toward sex. I wanted it more. With her of course. But after we broke up, all my relationships since have been sexually active.

I love sex and have become what people would call "kinky." I like experimenting now. Trying new things. I also fell in love with the female body. I love the way a woman looks naked, (and with clothes on as well, of course) But what I mean is I wouldn't describe myself as lustful but more like I appreciate the way a beautiful woman's body looks.

Looking back, I don't feel anything really. I don't regret it. It's all experience. And I'm glad I got it early in life because my girlfriends now enjoy having sex and I can tell their reactions are genuine.

I wouldn't change anything.

My advice is don't get addicted!

I heard about sex from my straight friends that it was a normal thing and that made me feel like a total outcast because it just didn't interest me and even "grossed me out." I didn't know what was "wrong" with me being so different.

[2]Female: I am 39.

I have to start by saying I'm a lesbian and the concept of losing my virginity may be different to the posed questions but it is my definition because that is my life. I was twenty-one when I had my first sexual experience and orgasm.

I had no expectations of what it would be like because I had an unusually sheltered concept of sex and never "went there" either physically or mentally. I just felt shut off to the whole idea for all of my teenage life. I assume this is because I was really gay and never knew what that meant.

She was my best friend at the time, who I was obviously in love with. I knew her for about six months and we had a crazy intensity between us and all I knew at the time was that I needed to be around her and in a desperate and crazy way I was drawn to her. She was nineteen and was experienced sexually with men and women. I knew her about six to eight months before I first had sex with her.

My parents never advised me on sex in any way. It was a topic in general that was never addressed and that gave me the idea that it wasn't supposed to happen or be discussed. Again that fit in my practice of shutting it off or shoving it under the rug.

I heard about sex from my straight friends that it was a normal thing and that made me feel like a total outcast because it just didn't interest me and even "grossed me out." I didn't know what was "wrong" with me being so different. I felt very embarrassed by not being interested in sex. I felt like a child in an adult world.

[2] This story is the one that moved us to construct a separate questionnaire for gay people. To the author of this piece, we give a big thank you.

I did not get any advice from any religious figures. I am Jewish and never heard of sex through any Rabbis. I find it strange now that no one talked about sex to me while I was growing up. I had some uncomfortable situations by men in authority positions like teachers, bosses, etc. and they added to my sense that it was this other awful world that I wanted nothing to do with. I do wish now that it had been addressed by my parents, my Rabbi and the world in general as far as the option that I might be gay. The world is a different place now and I know that would have saved me all the years of not knowing it myself and therefore depression and psychotherapy.

It happened in her bed while I was sleeping over one night. I didn't know it would happen and it totally took me by surprise. I didn't even understand the sensations my body was feeling. It was like I never heard of the idea and I had no idea what was going on other than it felt really good.

> *If homosexuality is a disease, let's all call in queer to work: "Hello. Can't work today, still queer."*
> *–Robin Tyler*
> Source: www.quotegarden.com

All of the next questions do not pertain to me so I'm not sure how to answer them. I'm trying to answer this questionnaire in an honest and personal way on a question that is really just for heterosexuals. That leaves out many people and I think it's important that all sorts of people answer this. I'm bypassing the guidelines but keeping it honest for my situation. I feel the same way when people ask me if I'm married. The answer is always "No, I'm gay." It's like a question that doesn't fit or assumes a whole other world. Okay, I will continue to answer now.

She was gentle and sweet as a nineteen year old could be. She tried to explain to me what was going on in my body and wanted to please me.

The best part was that I began to find myself in a whole new way, connecting me with my insides. The worst part was how foreign it all felt and that was very scary. How I felt for her was intensified after that and I wanted more. I soon realized I wanted a monogamous relationship because I loved her so much and that was never her plan. For her, being with a woman was recreation. I soon found it to be the most painful relationship in my life.

I told my aunt and her reaction was just happiness that I had been sexual of any sort. She screamed out "Did you have an orgasm?" I was very lucky to have such support at the time.

She is now married with two children and we grew apart and are no longer in touch. I could find her if I wanted to. I know where she is but it seems silly to be in touch now when we don't have anything in common anymore.

I look back at that experience as setting the tone of intensity for love and sex. It is not so helpful or adult to seek out love to match this intense pace and that is something I'm still learning. It won't always be as huge as that time.

The only thing I would change if I could is that I had more understanding of my body and being gay and what that meant. I think coming from such an unknowing place to feeling all that pent up desire for so long made the experience so extreme for me. It set a precedent that cannot be lived up to and has confused sex with knowing myself. Much of my experience was affected by being gay in a world that wasn't yet gay knowledgeable. My virginity wasn't just physical: It was all the other levels of self knowledge as well. It was my first experience to knowing that part of me and usually that is felt way before the actual first time of "going all the way."

I *felt bad for her afterwards and we didn't speak to each other for a few days.*

[3]Male: I am 40 years old. I just turned 13 when I first had sex with my neighbor girlfriend at the time.

I didn't have expectations that I remember. I recall my friends telling me stories of their brothers etc. At this point in my life I was pretty naïve about a lot of things.

She was a girl named Janine and was a neighbor that lived next door to me. We were the same age, went to school together and played together. We explored our neighborhood, hid in the neighbor's garage a lot and made out. She was very developed for a girl that age and I recall she wore a full B cup. So I became very fast and skillful at removing a bra. I was actually caught by my mom removing Janine's bra once.

Janine and I lived next to each other for a good year before we lost our virginity to each other. It was a process of getting to know each other until we actually were inseparable. Oh, my mom was the most concerned about our hanging out an awful lot and she was always telling me to behave and respect Janine. My father, on the other hand, was a redneck, so for him guys should do their best to bed a woman or girl, or at least get to first base and second if it was within grasp. I know my dad liked that I hung out with her a lot and even would ask if I kissed her yet. Of course most of the rumors I heard were all false. My buddies and I would get hard and show off our dicks to each other, truth or dare, but of those who said they had had sex, I never believed them. Guys are all talk, especially at twelve to thirteen years of age. My friends would tell me they would watch their sisters in the shower or their parents have sex. But that was the extent of it.

I wasn't religious and didn't get any advice there.

We actually did it in her parents' garage on a mattress on the floor.

[3] This is a story we found disturbing but included it because we felt there was merit in it. If anything like this ever happens to you or to someone you know, the authorities should be notified. The father in this story was a sick man and to this day, we can't help but wonder about his daughter and what she may have endured at his hands.

Her dad knew that we were always kissing and actually was encouraging us to strip and he wanted to film us but we would run out of the room. Back then I thought he was kidding to scare us from kissing. Until one night when I was taking out the trash, I saw him standing on a ladder filming his daughter in the tub. When he saw me, he told me to be silent or he would make me sorry I saw him. Because we were pressured from her father, we actually succumbed and when we did finally commit and have sex, I was both very, very scared and excited. I was hard immediately, we giggled like crazy and squirmed to the point where we would break into laughter until I entered her and pushed in and out about two times and stopped. She said it hurt too much and I was done with the moment.

We didn't use birth control, just natural. It was both exciting for me that first time and scary too. I remember my heart pounding in fear my dad would walk in and beat us silly. Her dad was really nice to us, spoke softly. I won't forget his voice and how soft he was directing us to do the act correctly. It actually felt very warm to my penis. I had had oral sex before but that was my first intercourse and I will always remember the very, very warm feeling and also the sounds in the garage seemed distant, like I was listening to something from far away. I remember the smell of the old station wagon parked along side the mattress.

I was excited and nervous that my dad would find us and I have to say I enjoyed her father looking at me nude and erect. Nobody had ever seen me naked and erect before. Janine had but not an adult. I was respectful the whole time because she was my best friend and I would like to say I was gentle but it all happened so fast and we were giggling, so I don't recall that exactly.

She knew what her dad wanted from her, so she was scared and excited too. We had history with being naked before and touching but nothing as intimate as intercourse, so she was nervous and curious, as I was.

The trouble I had getting it in was only with my balance, her father kind of gave step by step instructions and I remember pushing too hard at first to enter. That did hurt her now that I think about it.

The best part was the experience of the warmth for the first time and actually having her father examining me nude and hard. The worst part was the way I felt afterward. I felt ashamed for a while and dirty. I remember dressing and running home and taking a shower.

At first I was embarrassed and I had the feeling for a few days, then at the same time I was proud of myself because I did the MAN THING. My friends and I would call it doing the MAN THING. I never regretted what happened and still don't, because it was what it was at that time in my life. I felt bad for her afterwards and we didn't speak to each other for a few days. When we did, we kind of looked at each other for a few minutes and laughed. She made me promise not to talk about it. I didn't tell anyone. It was our secret and I never did tell my friends. I valued Janine's friendship and didn't want to break that bond between us.

I don't know what happened to her. My family moved about two months later and I never saw her again.

I chose to lose my virginity with her because of circumstance, pressure from her father and curiosity. This experience never put a negative feeling toward sex for me. It actually, after I moved, made me more curious about sex.

Looking back, I feel fine and don't regret my life. I would not change what I did. I think it helped me to understand me better and made me look at what turns me on more. It was all good actually.

Advice is: Wait until you find the person you want to experience love with and use protection. But enjoy the feeling and make it last.

It was a fun going back over distant memories.

1965 *The age of lost innocence brought on by the assassination of JFK and the Vietnam War. Our guys were dying over there. The music was telling us our souls were all one and it was time to love one another right now.*

Female:

I am 54. I have two daughters and three grandchildren. The age I was then is not as important as the age of what was happening—where we were as a society. 1965. The age of lost innocence brought on by the assassination of JFK and the Vietnam War. Our guys were dying over there. The music was telling us our souls were all one and it was time to love one another right now. The Beatles had invaded. All of it was happening so fast and it was time to keep up or get out of the way.

I was fifteen. I don't remember expectations. I think I wanted to make changes and adjustments to myself and that seemed like a good one. I just wanted to. His name was Bobby. He was nineteen and a virgin too. I met him cruising on Ventura Blvd. at the root beer stand. I was with an older girl who had a car. I liked him a lot. He was cute and polite. He grew up along the Gulf of Mexico and was an only child of a car salesman and a food worker. He worked as a valet at a club in Hollywood AND had held the Oscar won by Julie Christie that year for Best Actress. Well, that took my breath away. He had blond hair and blue eyes and made me giggle and made me feel older. He had a 1962 Impala and a 1049 Harley David-son. WOW! We decided together to do it. All of his friends were older. They all had motorcycles and we went riding every weekend.

We were having trouble getting our parts to match up. We would get naked and kiss and do other stuff and then he would put it somewhere in the general area and—nothing. We could not get it. We had heard of girls popping their cherries on the back of bikes over bumps. So on our rides he would say, "Clamp down, here comes a railroad track or a bump." But that didn't work, of course. Finally we figured it out and it really surprised us, even though we had been aiming for it. There was so much blood that he got scared and insisted that we go to my house and wake up my mom and tell her what was going on. I was so embarrassed but my mom was very cool and said all was normal. She took me the doctor soon after and all was well. He put the bed sheet in his car and left it there until it started to stink and I told him to throw it away.

The last I heard of him he married a woman a lot older than him with two kids. He also gained a lot of weight. I stayed friends with his mom for several years and then lost touch. I have always chosen nice men to be with because of him. He was so sweet and caring that I have made that a top priority with partners.

*S*he *could read me like a book and took pity on me. She knew I had never "done it" and, of course, I had my damned tongue hanging out my mouth all the time—and one day she leaned toward me, put her hand on my cheek, looked into my eyes and I just kissed her.*

Male: I am 65. I was 19

I was just really needy. I was anxious to do it, not scared but I didn't want to mess up. I was really horny. When I was about fifteen or sixteen, I'd almost had the chance but events conspired against me. We lived next door to these people who had a daughter who was younger than me. We had necked and petted but that's as far as it went. They also had a married daughter who lived in another state. She got divorced and came home to stay with her parents. She was nice looking, kind of countrified and she made an assignation with me. I had a paper route and I was to meet her after I was finished. I was getting ready to go and my father stopped me. He sensed something was up, I don't know how. He said, "I'm not stopping you but that woman across the way has been married, is used to sex and has been deprived of it for some time. If you go over there, you know what's going happen." I played dumb but how could I go then, when my dad knew what I was up to? I simply could not imagine (or rather I could imagine) him a few feet away, knowing exactly where, when and what I was doing. I just wasn't up to that, so I didn't meet her. She was pissed and I was frustrated for more than three more years.

When I finally did have sex it was with the mother of the girl I was in love with but who had no sexual interest in me. I'd known the mother about six months. She was forty-two and knew I was in love with her daughter. She really was a hell of a good sport and actually tried to foster a relationship between her daughter and me but it didn't come to anything.

She could read me like a book and took pity on me. She knew I had never "done it" and, of course, I had my damned tongue hanging out my mouth all the time—and one day she leaned toward me, put her hand on my cheek, looked into my eyes and I just kissed her.

We had to plot to avoid her husband. She said "There's always cars parked out by the university. You go and park and I'll come." I think she was horny, she knew I was needy and maybe it was an adventure for her. She was a good old gal, real pert, great personality. Her husband was ugly and fat. I couldn't understand at the time how or why she had ever married him. Now I'm an elderly gent and I know people change.

As for advice from my parents, there really wasn't anything useful.

My father was born in 1889, an Englishman during the reign of Queen Victoria. In terms of sexual attitudes, he was a living anachronism. What I got from him was that nice girls didn't do it until they were married. Once I drew a picture of a nude woman. I was maybe twelve years old when I drew it. My parents found it. I didn't have everything in the right place but it was all there. My father's reaction was to have a fit. I was a filthy guttersnipe. My mother, who was about twenty-five years younger than my father, had a completely different reaction. She didn't say anything, just went to take a bath and called me in with some excuse about not having any soap or something. She never talked but she made sure I knew how a woman was built. And that was it. No advice.

My friends were just as uninformed as I was. When I was twelve or thirteen, we would have Junior Assembly dances. I would ballroom dance—not close. There was this girl a year older than me and she was good looking. I asked her to dance. She grabbed me and just put herself right up next to me and I popped an instant hard-on. I tried to pull away and spent the rest of the dance with my ass sticking out. I was horribly embarrassed. The kids in those days were talking about using a jock strap to keep your dick from sticking out and embarrassing you. Of course, that was pretty academic, because that wouldn't really do the job. I was dumb enough to mention my problem to my dad. He told me I had a dirty mind and ought not to go to dances if I couldn't control myself any better than that.

I didn't get any advice from religious figures. I wasn't a churchgoer and would never have had the nerve to mention it to a minister or priest, considering my own dad's inability to empathize.

We did it in a parked car in an overgrown wooded area about twenty miles out of town, off the highway where even the ruts ended, in front of a barbed wire fence. It was about 11 pm. We got into the back seat and when I had the mechanics of position figured out and was about to enter her a panther screamed nearby. I said, "What the hell was that?" and she told me. A panther's scream is a high-pitched soprano. It sounded exactly like a woman screaming at the top of her lungs. The difference is that a woman, after screaming like that, would continue to make noises—sobbing, etc. When it's a panther, the scream is followed by dead silence. It's a pretty eerie thing. Normally it would have made the hair stand up on the back of my neck, especially in the woods in the middle of the night and in total darkness. Under the circumstances, however, with my penis touching her orifice, it could have been a charging bull elephant and it wouldn't have been much of a distraction.

At first I was awkward to the point of needing guidance finding the place and being afraid to hurt her. I had to be told, "Ted, you aren't giving me as much as you can." I was so ignorant that I had only been using about half because I was afraid that the whole thing would hurt her. After her comment I was very quickly disabused of that notion. She was incredibly kind and very gentle with my feelings. She was very appreciative and built my ego by showing me and telling me how much she enjoyed it, though she was very genteel about it.

The best part was that I was both giving and getting intense pleasure. I can't say I was surprised about anything about the act itself. I had been building up to it for such a long time. By then I had stimulated myself manually for years and was no stranger to climax. Maybe I was a little surprised about how good I felt but I was mostly relieved and gratified and—yes—proud, because she made it obvious that I had done well. We didn't use any birth control because she told me she'd had a hysterectomy. Because of the circumstances I had a certain amount of guilt, her being a married woman and the deception involved. However, it felt absolutely WONDERFUL and I was considerably better off for it in mind and body.

There was no worst part other than the stab of guilt because she was married. Other than that there was no down side for me.

I remember a sort of enhanced feeling: of having arrived at manhood. There was pride that I had been able to provide pleasure to her. In fact, that was even more important to me than my own physical sensations—that I had the power to cause pleasure. It can and should be a power trip in the finest and most generous sense.

I never mentioned it specifically to anyone that I can remember, at least not for many years and if I have, it was a cursory, generalized account.

She died a few years ago.

I chose to lose my virginity at that time with that woman because I could. I was so needy and she was ready to give me what I needed. I will always be grateful for her gift to me. My attitude towards sex is a good one, I think, because of her and it's lasted a lifetime.

I wouldn't change a thing because it was just about perfect. What would have been better but WAY more complicated and dangerous and fraught with emotional peril would have been if it had actually happened with the girl who was the object of my affection. Odds are, though, it would have been worse with all the emotional land mines. This way was simply a gift.

My advice to virgins would be to find a kind, experienced, somewhat older woman who is not foolish enough to become emotionally involved. Ben Franklin was right in spades.[4]

[4] We Googled Ben Franklin and found that on June 25, 1745, he'd written a letter to a friend advising him to "prefer old women to young ones". A reprint of the letter is at the back of this book.

Mom knocked and came in my room searching through it and found him in the closet.

Female: I'm 20 years old. I was 12, turning 13 in a few days.

I wanted it to be like making love to the person that I loved and it was. He was my first boyfriend and I thought he would be my one and only. He was thirteen at the time.

I'd known him since fifth grade but we became friends in sixth grade, where I had a crush on him and we finally got together as boyfriend and girlfriend in the seventh grade. I lost my virginity that summer right before eighth grade.

My parents didn't know but they found out because he sneaked over one night and my Mom knocked and came in my room searching through it and found him in the closet. Obviously, she had been suspecting that things were going on. So when she found out she freaked. She gave me the whole "I'm disappointed in you" lecture and told me that my virginity was supposed to be saved for the man I would marry and that

no man would want to marry me if they found out that I wasn't a virgin anymore. I felt bad, like I failed her, yet I had no regret about losing my virginity to my first boyfriend.

Rumors were that girls who lost their virginity were easy because the boys would brag about it but my boyfriend never would admit that I lost my virginity to him. My friend knew but everyone kept it on the down low.

No religious advice but there was this one time I thought I missed my period and we went to a free pregnancy place and the lady there had a whole talk about God forgiving and that I could declare a second virginity.

I lost it in my bedroom. I was expecting it because we had been talking about it for a while, then it finally happened. We used a condom: We couldn't afford to get me pregnant.

I felt happy and tingly inside and my heart just weakened as he put it in.

He was very cautious. He didn't want to hurt me in any way, was very gentle and the feeling of it was sweet. He had a little trouble getting his penis in but I think most people do.

The best part was just being there with him and doing this because at the time he was my everything and I know I was his. I guess the worst part was just when he first put it in because it did hurt a little: He had to take his time and slowly put it in.

Overall, I felt good, no regrets, not awkward and most important, I felt loved. He didn't just get off me and go to sleep. He told me he loved me, kissed me and held me in his arms as we fell asleep. I felt that I loved him and sex was a way of showing that affection.

I didn't tell anyone immediately after. I think my cousin was the first to know; maybe about a month after it had happened. This was business between my boyfriend and me and I didn't feel the need to share that with the whole world.

We broke up freshmen year in high school around December. He wasn't showing the kind of affection I was looking for, or maybe I just lost interest. I wanted to see other people. We remained good friends afterwards until my junior year and that was it. I haven't talked to him since because of some things that happened. He totally changed. He wasn't anything like the person that I had fallen in love with and I finally realized it and we ended the friendship then.

I chose to lose my virginity with him because I felt that I did love him and I saw a future for the two of us in the long run. Call me silly or stupid but I thought that he would be my husband in the future and the father of my children. We even named our eggs in Home Economics Teen Living as if they were going to be our kids' real names.

After he and I broke up, I didn't want to get serious with anyone else. I guess because I lost my virginity to him, I didn't want to move on. I thought that maybe one day we would get back together.

I look back and think of it as a learning experience. We were kids doing grown up things because we were curious. I know that I did love him at the time and I don't regret him to be my first but we were only kids when this happened.

I wouldn't change any part of it because it was mutual and we both wanted to go through with it. However, for selfish reasons, I would have liked saving my virginity for the man that I am with now because he was a virgin when we began to have sex but then again, that wasn't the situation that was meant to be.

Your virginity is one of the most precious things that you have. Don't just give it away to anyone because one day when you look back, you don't want to regret it. As hard as it is, try not be to pressured into it because if you feel pressure, more than likely you're probably not ready for it.

A̶fterwards I started worrying about if I got an STD from her or if I got her pregnant but it passed.

Male: I am 23. I was 18.

I had no clue what it was going to be like. I just wanted it.

She was in a couple of my classes. I knew who she was for years. We weren't best friends or anything.

The advice from my parents was that if I was going to have sex, use a condom. My brother explained to me what a condom was. I really don't remember any advice from friends. I'm not religious so I didn't get any advice there.

We did it at a party in an upstairs bedroom. It wasn't a planned thing. She was talkin' dirty. I took her up on it. I used a condom. Afterwards I started worrying about if I got an STD from her or if I got her pregnant but it passed. Let's just say it was quick. I got the feeling she was a little disappointed. I didn't have trouble trying to get it in. She was experienced.

The sex part was the best, the worst was thinking of all the stuff that could happen. I felt a little regret that I should have waited for someone I cared about. I didn't really feel anything for her because it was just a spur of the moment thing.

> *In 2008, there were more than 1.5 million total cases of chlamydia and gonorrhea reported to CDC—making them the two most commonly reported infectious diseases in the United States*
>
> Source: www.cdc.gov

I told all my friends afterward.

I am unsure of what happened with her. She left town after graduation and I never saw her again.

I chose to have sex with her because I was an eighteen-year-old boy! HORMONES!!!

I wish I wouldn't have been drinking at the party. I would have wanted to do it with someone special.

My advice to virgins is DON'T WAIT, MASTURBATE

The only advice I got from Mom was "Don't get yourself into trouble."

Female: I am 39 years of age. I was 22 at the time.

I wanted it to be amazing, feel really good and have a connection with my partner.

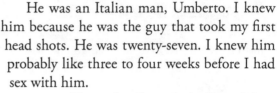

He was an Italian man, Umberto. I knew him because he was the guy that took my first head shots. He was twenty-seven. I knew him probably like three to four weeks before I had sex with him.

The only advice I got from Mom was "Don't get yourself into trouble." Dad was deceased. My friends told me that it was a good thing and you can have fun but use protection. I was not brought up religious. I don't like church. My church was the ballet theatre, so there was no religious input.

We did it in his apartment. It wasn't very pretty. The bed was not comfortable. I knew it would happen because European men are pretty straightforward if you go home with them. I took my friend's advice and we used a condom.

It was weird. I really didn't relax and there was no orgasm because I didn't even know what an orgasm felt like. It was a little painful but not that bad; more disconnected. I think he thought I wasn't a virgin so he just wanted a roll in the hay. I was a little scared after and a little during but mostly after because I didn't realize you can become connected more to the person, especially if you are attracted to them. I think that was the scariest for me. I found myself with emotions I'd never experienced for a man, especially because I grew up with pretty much women and the ballet world, which had a mixed crowd.

He was respectful but he was not so gentle. Probably because I didn't tell him I was a virgin. So it was awkward. He was not sweet, he was kind of matter of fact, like "Let's go to bed now. "

It only hurt a little but because of so much stretching from dancing I was pretty okay with that and the control.

The best part was that I got that far with him because I really liked him. The worst part was he wasn't as sweet and kind as I thought. It wasn't as beautiful as it should have been.

I felt good about myself afterward but at the same time I had to hide it from my mom because she was very much opposed to sex before marriage, so I did feel guilt and fear that she would find out but she knew anyway. Moms always have a way of knowing. However I didn't regret it at all. I was proud. I liked him but didn't trust him because he was only in this country for a short time.

I told some girlfriends, a couple women I danced with.

He went back to Italy. I went once to visit, which was not good. He tried to strangle me and he also had a girlfriend. He was horrible. I left for Paris very quickly. He called me a few times after but think I only talked to him twice. I think he is still a photographer. I don't know. He would be forty-two or something.

I chose to be with him at that time in my life because all my friends had already had sex and I found a guy who I was really attracted to. He seemed like he knew what he was doing.

My views changed about sex because we started having a sexual relationship and he gave me my first orgasm and we also did a lot of experimenting with places and ways to do it. It was fun but all new. I guess it made me think that sex and a real relationship are two separate things and that men and women think differently about the feelings one has after you connect like that. I still think that way but a mature man would be able to have sexual and emotional feelings for you if he really likes you.

I look back on it as a jump into adulthood because unless you plan to be a nun, that experience is needed for your body and mind. God made us so that we experience this between a man and woman, so I guess the feelings are already implanted.

What I would change is who I lost it with, someone who would have been sweet and kind and all that but I was scared of the emotional attachment with this guy. Maybe it seemed safer in that way (emotionally). It didn't mess with my emotions, just the act. I guess I didn't realize the emotional attachment you can get and I ended up getting hurt because of the fear of connecting on a higher level.

My advice would be to wait until you feel good about the actual act and yourself also. Be aware of men that only have sex to offer you. Know the guy. Talk to him. Ask him questions and be sure he is kind. Of course use a condom or some kind of birth control. Be safe. Have fun!

*F*or the most part it was more of a medal to lose your virginity, something that was to make you a man.

Male: I am 29 years old and single. I was 16 years of age, a junior in high school.

I always believed that I would lose my virginity to a girlfriend in school, someone who was my age. I had a belief that losing your virginity would be something special, romantic and would happen in a relationship. I lost my virginity to a twenty-nine year old married woman, who was a friend of the family. She was also was a neighbor for whom I babysat her three children and worked part time for her husband during the summer and on weekends during the school year. I knew her probably for about two years.

My parents never really talked to me about losing my virginity and they could never find out 'til this day who I lost my virginity to. My family and her family had a falling out and do not speak anymore. From my friends I heard how great it was but for the most part it was more of a medal to lose your virginity, something that was to make you a man. Never really any advice. I had no advice from a religious figure.

My first time was in her bedroom, a normal place, in the bed. He worked nights. I did not expect it to happen: She actually came home very early by herself from a night out when I was babysitting. She grabbed my crotch and kissed me. She then told me how she felt. It just went from there. Pretty risky and pretty exciting. She did have a condom in a drawer and made me use it. I'm not sure about the type of condom.

Surprisingly, I was not nervous at all. I'd had a crush on her for quite awhile and always fantasized about it. She was a very attractive woman, with a great body for someone with three children. I remember thinking how I was the luckiest kid in the world but I did feel pressure to not mess it up and to perform well. I guess you can say it made me very happy that this was happening.

I have always been a respectful person to this day and I was definitely a gentleman at the age of sixteen, even though some would think the situation didn't call for gentle and sweet.

She enjoyed it very much and didn't believe that I was a virgin. I told her I watched a lot of pornographic movies and learned from that but she didn't believe me. I didn't have any trouble at all getting it in.

The best part was a feeling that I never felt before: those first thrusts into a woman, something you just don't know what it would be like if you never had done it before. The worst part was the fear of getting caught by someone, which was always in the back of my mind.

I guess being sixteen and getting an older woman who you lusted over and thought about (someone you thought you could never have) gave me a sense of pride. No regret now and no regret then. I actually had a crush on her, so I really liked her.

I told almost all of my friends. How could I not? 'Til this day it's a great story to tell.

We continued to sleep with each other for four months. She's still married, still lives in the same place but we do not speak.

I chose to lose my virginity at that time with her because my hormones were raging then, as they still are now and a fantasy was coming true. No girl my age had experience like her and no girl my age could do for me what she was doing for me—teaching me everything I didn't know.

I think in a way it sort of gave me the impression that sex wasn't just for relationships but sex was okay with anyone. You can say that in a way I felt I was more experienced than someone my age and that sex could be recreational.

I look back now and say I would never change what I did. It made me a man but I do regret that it was someone's wife. But on the other hand, it also gives me a bit of pride. I would never change anything that happened to me in my life. Everything happens for a reason and makes me who I am today.

The only advice I could really give is make sure you are comfortable and not just doing it to do it. It should be an enjoyable experience with someone whose company you enjoy.

P*hysically, my first sexual experience was painful. I don't remember him having trouble getting it in but I felt as though my body was being ripped in half.*

Female: I am 20. I was just 17.

He was my high school boyfriend of ten months. I was completely in love with him. He was fifteen. I had known of him for a few years but we had been dating for ten months.

My mom always said to wait until I felt that it was right and that I loved the person. From my friends I heard that it was painful, that it cleared one's complexion and that it changed the relationship forever. I had no religious advice at all.

We did it in my boyfriend's bedroom. I knew it was going to happen and I finally felt ready. I'd had it in my head for as long as I knew what sex was. I think the idea started with the Prom episode of *Beverly Hills 90210* when Brenda and Dylan finally took their relationship to the next level. Like Brenda, I pictured it being my prom night. In a gorgeous hotel room on a bed laced with rose petals, I would lose my sacred virginity to my special someone. In reality, my first time having sex was not out of any TV show but it was one of the most amazing experiences of my life.

During high school, I dated Jim for three years. He was sweet, smart and handsome and had big plans for his future. He was great but two years younger than me, which caused some issues in our small school. However, we did not let it get in our way. Since we were both pretty inexperienced, our physical relationship progressed in steps. This made every new level more intimate and special. Being that we moved at such a gradual pace, sex was not even mentioned until we had been together for at least six months. I had so many fears and concerns. Every time we uttered the one syllable word, I would become so flustered that we just put it away again.

Looking back, my worries were not what really stopped me. I just was not ready. I worried about it changing our relationship, pregnancy, the pain of the first actual time and about Jim. However, when we did have sex for the first time, I did not even think twice about any of these things. So this short list of concerns was only my way of stalling.

On a rainy day in the end of March, ten months into our relationship, we sat in the high school gym discussing our day, when one of us brought up the topic of sex. For a while we had avoided this word but somehow on this ordinary day it snuck back into our minds. After a brief conversation the two of us realized that we no longer knew what was holding us back anymore. So on that day we found ourselves on his bed with a box of condoms and a bigger box of nerves. As we began to fool around, the idea of what was to come seemed to seep away from us. After a while, Jim asked me once more if I was positive that I was ready. Even with how nervous I was, I still knew that I wanted to share this with him, so I said yes.

Physically, my first sexual experience was painful. I don't remember him having trouble getting it in but I felt as though my body was being ripped in half. In an overwhelming mixture of physical pain and unfathomable emotional connection, I cried. With every tear that spilled out from my eyes, Jim kept kissing me and telling me he loved me. Though he asked countless times if I wanted to stop, I knew that I wanted to be right there with him.

Afterward I felt emotionally vulnerable. I experienced such a mixture of emotions. I loved him more. I felt more attached to him. I felt more vulnerable. However, to this day I have never regretted losing my virginity to him.

I didn't tell anyone for at least six months after. It was such a personal event that I didn't feel close enough to anyone that I wanted to share this amazing thing with them.

We still talk but when we broke up I was really hurt by our ending. Though he remains one of the most important people in my life, I find it very hard to stay his close friend.

Being very close to my mom, I took her advice and realized she probably knew what she was talking about. I wanted my first time to be special and one that I would not later regret. I loved him and I wanted to share this with him. I also wanted our relationship to have a lasting effect on him. I know losing his virginity to me was a very important moment in his life that he still quotes as one of the best.

This experience made me realize how amazing sex could be with someone you care for so much. To this day, I find it important to have sex with those that mean something to me. I would never judge or not understand why anyone has a one night stand but I know that it is just not for me.

Remembering my first time still puts a smile on my face. It does make me a bit teary sometimes. However, I am glad that this physically painful experience is finally done. I don't think that there is a single part of it that I would change.

My advice to virgins would be to make it meaningful. One of the worst feelings is regret. Don't make this an event that leaves you with that feeling.

If a boy got a girl pregnant he would have to marry her. Then he would have to financially support the girl, the baby and himself.

> **Merriam-Webster's Collegiate Dictionary Tenth Edition defines "virgin" in part as: virgin...**
> **1a: an unmarried woman devoted to religon.**
> **2a: an absolutely chaste young woman**
> **b: an unmarried girl or woman...**
> **4a: a person who has not had sexual intercourse b: a person who is inexperienced in a usu. specified sphere of activity**
> **5: a female animal that has never copulated**

Male: I'm 75.

First of all, let me say that the whole concept of virginity is something I have a great deal of difficulty with. Until recently, I never thought of virginity as something that could be applied to a male. I'm a history buff and historically, in the reading I've done virginity was something that was only referred to when it involved a female. We heard about the Virgin Mary but never about a Virgin Joseph, or even a Virgin Jesus. The Roman Vestal Virgins were all women attending a female Goddess. (At least the assumption is that the Virgins were all women—they are never identified as female virgins, only as virgins but I don't think anyone has ever suggested that some or all were males.) In more recent historical times virginity was a concept that men used in regard to young women as a part of the cultural belief that women were considered to be property—first belonging to their fathers and later to their husbands. Within this framework, a woman who was a virgin before marriage was regarded as having more value than one who was not. So I never really liked the concept of virginity and never thought of that status as having any meaning for me as a male.

Another reason I never thought of virginity in personal terms is that the meaning of the term really seems to make no sense. Who or what IS a "virgin" anyway? The meaning has usually had a sexual connotation but rather than being defined as sexual activity or behavior, it has tended to be defined in the narrow sense of penetration of a vagina by a penis. It's such a narrow and limited definition that, for me, it has no real meaning. Consider: A twelve-year-old girl is the victim of a rape. There was nothing sexual about the encounter and she did not participate in the act. Has she "lost" her virginity? Penetration took place but nothing more. To say she's no longer a virgin is a travesty. How about a man or woman whose sexual experiences have been all with the same sex? He/she has never experienced "intercourse" in the sense of penetration but has had several "lovers" and has engaged in sexual acts leading up to orgasm many times. Or a heterosexual couple who have engaged in frequent sex-play including mutual masturbation, oral sex, etc., etc. with orgasms? Or, finally, a girl who has never had a penis inserted in her vagina but has inserted other objects such as a dildo, vibrator or even a tampon and has eliminated her hymen? Are all these individuals still virgins? According to the narrow definition, yes. To me, these examples make the whole concept of virginity meaningless.

When I was growing up and beginning to have sexual feelings and engage in sexual behavior, I never really thought about being a virgin. I was very shy and very insecure in terms of male-female relationships and was never sexually attracted to males. I was short and in those days (1940s and 1950s) no girl who was even somewhat attractive wanted to be seen in

Statistics show that approximately 90% of men and 65% of women masturbate from time to time.
~ Kanner, Bernice. 2005. Are You Normal About Sex, Love and Relationships?
La Vergne, TN: Lightning Source, Inc.
Source: www.randomhistory.com

public with a boy who was shorter than she was. So I was very "retarded" in terms of having girlfriends, dating, etc. We fellows knew that some of our classmates "did it" but I don't ever remember thinking that someone's virginity had been "lost."

I remember that in my high school class of about sixty-five students, two girls got pregnant during the four years we were in school together. Both immediately married their boyfriends and that was the factor that was of overriding importance in my mind. The fear of causing a pregnancy was far more meaningful to me than any thought about the esoteric concept of losing one's virginity—whatever that was. If a boy got a girl pregnant he would have to marry her. Then he would have to financially support the girl, the baby and himself. Those realities of the times were always foremost in my thoughts when I was actually involved in a romantic relationship with a girl. I had had several summer jobs and hated them all. No way did I want to get myself into a situation where I'd have to get, and keep, a full time job. Going to school was a much easier and more satisfying life.

I only had one real girlfriend in high school. In my junior year—I was sixteen or seventeen at the time—I began going out with a girl a year behind me in school. Jane lived with her parents on their farm a few miles out of town. I don't remember the circumstances of how we started going out together. She was a pretty dark-haired girl about my height. I had learned to masturbate several years earlier. So I was aware of sex and of sexual feelings.

Jane and I developed a routine on our dates. My parents would let me take their car and I would drive out to Jane's home and pick her up. We would drive around for a while, maybe go to a movie. I don't recall that there was ever a curfew imposed on either of us. At some point I would find a spot on a back road, where there was room enough to pull off the road and park and where there was very little traffic. We would engage in kissing and what we referred to in those days as necking.

One night after we'd been dating for a month or two, I tried putting my hand on her breast. I think my motivation was curiosity more than any thing else. She made no objection, so in the course of the next half-hour or so I managed to get my hand under her sweater and then under her bra. I remember a feeling of exhilaration and happiness, that I was actually now moving from necking to petting. Jane seemed to enjoy it too. At least she made no objections.

Over the course of several dates we eventually evolved to the point of moving to the back seat of the car. In those days, cars mostly had bench type seats stretching the entire width of the car, in both front and back. We'd lie down on the back seat and continue kissing, necking and petting—today, I suppose that's what's known as making out. We went out together for over a year and this was how almost every date ended. Neither of us ever even attempted to touch the other below the waist—not once. I never considered the possibility of attempting intercourse. That had nothing to do with concern about virginity. It was just that I knew that could lead to pregnancy and there was no way I wanted to run that risk. To illustrate how uptight I was about sex in general, I was very embarrassed that Jane might notice that I had an erection and I didn't want that to happen. To hide this evidence of sexual arousal, I took to wearing an athletic supporter (jock strap) whenever we went out! Can you imagine? After I took Jane home, I would go home and masturbate.

My feelings and thoughts were of happiness and satisfaction in what we were doing. There was an intimacy that I found very pleasurable. I don't remember ever feeling frustrated because I wanted or hoped to go farther. I was quite content. Jane seemed to feel the same way. She never objected to what we were doing, nor did she ever indicate any desire or need to go beyond it. Of course, we never really talked about it, so I don't really know how she felt.

We finally broke up when a neighbor of hers came back from his two-year enlistment in the Navy and asked her out. She declined but soon after told me that she didn't want to go steady with me anymore. She said she still wanted to go out with me but that Joe, who was three years older than me, wanted to go out with her and she wanted to see him also. I remember thinking that this older guy who had spent two years in the Navy would be more aggressive in wanting to have real sex (intercourse) and I thought that Jane just might be persuaded. So I said no, it would have to be one or the other of us and so we broke up. A couple years later they were married.

That was my first experience with sex and even though I had no thoughts involving virginity, I don't think anyone would suggest that I'd lost mine.

I didn't have another real girlfriend until I was a senior in college. I was twenty-one. Her name was Judy and she was a music student, a year younger than I, known to be quite religious and not someone who was known to date. Mostly, when we went out together it was to college functions. I wasn't religious but I remember making an effort to go to church and even joined the Student Christian Association in an effort to please her. She had been hired to play the organ at a church in a neighboring town and I'd usually go with her. She never tried to push her religious ideas on me and I doubt if I would have continued seeing her if she had.

I'm not sure how long we'd been seeing each other—not too long, I think—and we'd done nothing sexual except the first base activity of kissing and necking. One day we been out for a drive and when we came back I stopped in front of my house. We were sitting in the front seat doing the usual first base activities. I'd gotten out of the car and gotten in on the passenger side so as to get out of the way of the steering wheel. Judy was wearing a sort of baggy sweatshirt and a pair of loose fitting blue jeans.

At some point the kissing got unusually passionate and I slipped my hand under her sweatshirt. I rather expected she might push my hand away or tell me not to do that. She made no objection, however. Encouraged and emboldened, I began feeling her breasts, first over her bra and then sliding her bra up to expose her breasts. Again she made no remonstrance. This was territory I was familiar with from times with Jane but I was older now and knew—from reading mainly—a little more about sexual behavior. Thinking that she would surely stop me this time, I decided to move on to unknown territory and slid my hand down over her stomach until I reached her waistband and tried to slip my hand underneath. I was both astonished and overjoyed when, instead of an angry demand to desist, she sucked in her stomach to make it easier for me to slide my hand inside both her jeans and her panties. For the first time I was exploring the sexual center of a girl. I felt like I had gone to heaven.

About that time I realized that I was not in heaven. Instead I was parked on a public street in broad daylight. It was not a busy street and no one had come by, either on foot or in a car but it was a pretty exposed position. I withdrew my hand and said something like, "Why don't we go inside?", motioning toward the house. I was an only child and my parents both worked so there would be no one there. Judy quickly agreed.

We went in, I led her to my room, we went in and I closed the door. Then I received the biggest and most wonderful shock of my life. I had, I think, expected that we would sit down on the edge of the bed where I could resume my somewhat timorous groping. Instead, as I turned to face Judy, she looked at me and said, "Should I take my clothes off?" I was nearly speechless. I'd not expected that, despite what had been happening in the car. The shades were drawn, the door was closed, no one was there but us and I managed to mumble, "Okay." She proceeded to quickly strip off her clothes and I quickly followed her lead.

Naked except for socks, she lay down on the bed and I followed, lying on top of her. We proceeded to begin simulating having intercourse, my penis wedged against her vaginal area. Suddenly the thought struck me. I knew that even a man's "pre-cum" contained sperm and that penetration, even without ejaculation, could result in pregnancy. There it was again— the old fear of causing a pregnancy that I knew neither of us wanted. I realized that even without intending to insert my penis, it could happen accidentally in the midst of a passionate embrace. So I got up and explained to Judy that not wanting to risk even a small chance of her getting pregnant that maybe I should keep my shorts on in order to prevent an accidental penetration. She said she thought that was a good idea. So I put them back on and we resumed our simulated sex.

After a while—maybe fifteen or twenty minutes, I wasn't keeping track—I rolled off and laying on my side beside her, put my hand over her mons and began rubbing her vaginal and clitoral area. I knew that women were able to have orgasms and I was thrilled when I was able to bring her to one after a short while. I don't remember anything being said by either of us but I grabbed some tissues from a box by the bed, rolled over an my back and she didn't hesitate to take my erection in her hand and masturbate me to an orgasm in a very few minutes.

That became the established pattern of our sexual activity. Oh, there was one other time where we tried something different. That was on the very last time we were together. We had parked on a back road where there was a large pull-off area and practically no traffic. After an interval of kissing and petting, I unzipped my jeans and took my penis out. I don't remember saying anything, just gently pushing her head in that direction. She seemed to know what to do and leaned down, took my penis in her hand, then into her mouth and began sucking on it. As I began to show signs of reaching an orgasm she lifted her head and said, "Don't come." I had no intention of not coming but didn't say anything, just gently pushed her head back down. She took my penis back in her mouth and sucked me to orgasm. If I have any regret about my relationship with Judy, it's that we didn't move on to that stage of sex sooner. I wish we had been more aware of oral sex and been able to share that intimacy and pleasure during the course of our relationship. It would have added a level of intimacy that we missed out on. That would have fit in well with the determination to not risk pregnancy.

I don't remember any time in our relationship when I had a great urge to go further and have intercourse with penetration. This was not from any thoughts or concerns about virginity, either mine or hers but simply from being determined not to risk a pregnancy. Also what we were doing was totally satisfying. As far as I was concerned, we were having sex and I was in heaven. The feeling of joyous intimacy was new and wonderful to me. I think she shared my feelings.

I'm sure we would have gone on to intercourse if we could have been sure of avoiding a pregnancy. The only method of contraception available to me was to use a condom. I'd never heard that word at that time—we referred to them as rubbers. The only place I knew of where I could get them was the local drugstore. It was a small town, the druggist knew me and he knew my parents, so I was far too embarrassed to try to purchase them there. It never occurred to me to go to a drugstore in a neighboring town but I think I would still have been too embarrassed to ask to buy them even from a stranger. I did not feel that I could ask Judy to get herself fitted with a diaphragm. Anyway, going beyond what we were doing seemed unnecessary.

As far as I am concerned Judy and I were having sex. And in my mind, now that I'm asked to describe how I lost my virginity, that was when and how it happened. When I first had intercourse it was with my wife-to-be, the night before our wedding! It was nothing remarkable. I was twenty-five by that time and she was twenty. Actually, she had engaged in intercourse the summer before, although I wasn't aware of it at the time. With the fear of pregnancy removed (we'd decided we wouldn't try to have a child right away but we wouldn't try to prevent that possibility either), it seemed that there was no longer a reason not to have intercourse. So we did. It was pleasurable but was not a defining point in my life. I didn't have any thoughts at the time that I was finally "a man," that I had finally "lost my virginity." It was just another new and pleasurable experience but the earth didn't shake the way it had that first time with Judy.

My only advice to virgins would be not to worry about it. Whether or not you're a virgin doesn't really matter. The status of being a virgin or non-virgin is of no real importance. As I tried to say in the opening paragraphs, even the definition of the word is ambiguous and unclear. To me the word has no meaning and therefore is of no importance. Don't let an ambiguous word define who you are. Be yourself.

I realized I wasn't straight at sixteen. I hadn't any idea there was another option besides straight. I desperately clung to the familiar for three full years before accepting my homosexuality.

Female: I am 24. I was 18.

I pictured it to be just like in the movies. Flattering lighting, entangled in white sheets, hands traveling over curves, backs arching, breath catching....

Her name was Nicole. She went to high school with me. She was on the drill team and I carried and set their props for competition. She was also eighteen. I knew her perhaps a year or so before we had sex.

I realized I wasn't straight at sixteen. I hadn't any idea there was another option besides straight. I desperately clung to the familiar for three full years before accepting my homosexuality.

As for parental advice, my dad was very supportive but told me not to get tied down while I was so young. I had an absolute lack of advice on sex with other women. Nicole, however, assumed that we received some sort of handbook. I had no advice at all from religious figures.

We did it on the pull-out sofa bed in my parents' den. It took me a bit by surprise.

I had already outed myself but she was, and continues to be, straight. I was incredibly nervous. There was so much pressure, especially since she assumed I'd been with many women before, that I knew what I was doing, etc. It was very awkward and she let me do all the work. I was worried that my parents might hear us but I was more worried about getting it right. I think I was gentle as I could be. Definitely very awkward. She was too sensitive to have an orgasm and I was too green to realize I could be gentler.

I think the entire experience, which lasted maybe fifteen minutes, was beautiful and terrible all at once. The best part was realizing I was actually doing something good to a girl. The worst part was laying next to her after she told me to stop, as she was too sensitive. Afterwards I felt...inadequate.

We were friends. Nothing more, nothing less.

Did I tell anyone afterwards? Oh, absolutely.

We're still friends, though not as close. We tried it one more time but didn't go through with it.

I chose to lose my virginity at that time with that person because it was all about timing and opportunity. I had just never had the opportunity with a woman before. I felt awkward about sex for a while—like I wasn't very good at it. But I got over it.

Now that I'm older, I look back on that experience and feel amused. And grateful. Without that experience, I'd probably still be a virgin to women. I wouldn't change a thing. It was perfect for what it was.

My advice to virgins is that it will be awkward. Just do your best!

Even with my hormones racing through my body, I kept thinking, "This is it?"

Male: I'm 24. I was 15.

I never really gave virginity much thought, getting laid was the only thing in mind. I guess that's what most fifteen-year-old guys think.

A friend and I thought that by hanging out in a library we'd get to know some hot girls. He was right. Our first day trying out this technique we met three girls: a tall, hot, blonde Swedish chick and her two all right looking friends. We got to know them at the library and then we managed to get them to come over to my place, which was only a block away. Two of them were fourteen and one said she was fifteen. I wound up with the one who said she was fifteen. We had sex the same day we met.

I don't remember my father ever really giving me any advice on sex or virginity or girls even. My mother mentioned condoms every now and again. From my friends, I kept hearing the usual, of how great it is. I never got any advice from them. Young guys really don't know much yet. I didn't get any advice from religious figures.

We did it in my neighbor's garage. It's where I'd spend most of my nights lifting weights or hanging out with friends.

When these chicks came over to my house I had no idea it would happen. They stayed at my place for about two hours or so and went home. The guy I was with received oral sex from the girl I wound up with, so I never imagined having sex with her. I left my apartment about an hour after and she was outside, so that totally took me by surprise. We didn't use any birth control.

It didn't feel as great as I had heard it would. Even with my hormones racing through my body, I kept thinking, "This is it?" A small part of me was very happy, however, only because of the basics: good looking girl, naked, having sex with me, losing my virginity—that kind of stuff. No big deal, probably because I had no experience and didn't know how to make it better.

> ## *Sex is God's joke on human beings.*
> *- Bette Davis*
> *Source: www.allgreatquotes.com*

It began by her giving me oral sex as well and telling me to pull her hair and things like that, so the respect went out the door almost right away. Plus she had just performed oral sex on my buddy and we all know what a girl like that is called in high school. When the sex began, I wasn't gentle at all; too rough I guess you can say. I later found out that she lost her virginity to me as well.

She urged me to do it. I guess I'd have to call and ask her a couple of questions to find out what her reaction was. I had a little trouble getting it in. Like I said, I found out later she was a virgin too.

The best part was seeing my penis in her vagina. I'll never forget that sight. The oral was awesome as well. The worst part was that the sex wasn't so great.

Afterwards, I was afraid for a while, being that I didn't use a condom. She told me she had sex with several other guys before me (a lie), so I was afraid of diseases. I felt like a dirty dog, honestly. After that day we messed around some but I never felt much toward her and it never led to anything. I didn't tell anyone about it. You're the first, believe it or not. I don't know what became of her. I lost contact with her a few months after that.

I chose to lose my virginity at that time with that girl because I was so horny and it didn't matter who she was. When I ran into her outside, she told me about how she gave my friend head and would like to give me some next. It was only natural, I believe, for me to have gotten hard as granite.

The experience didn't change anything in my thoughts about sex. I was a little kid! Being a freshman in high school, the only thing I had in mind was sex.

I still get horny sometimes when I think back on it. I think that if I could go back to that day, there would be a lot of things I would do differently. Wearing a condom for one. Making it a more enjoyable experience for another, instead of just having tried to make a hardcore fucking.

My advice to virgins is to take it easy and wear a condom. Waiting for "the one" is bullshit but definitely try to make the best of it.

I've come a long way since that day. I've learned that having sex with someone you love makes it even better.

I guess I saw it as more of a skill I needed to be familiar with in order to complete my femininity.

Female: I am 37. I was 21.

I came very close to losing my virginity at the age of eighteen to the twenty-two year old friend of a twenty-seven year old guy I had a crush on. I was too scared at the time. I remember him trying to seduce me and I was just going through the motions of allowing him to unzip my jeans and pull them down. When he actually tried to put himself inside me, I was petrified of how much it would hurt. He saw how scared I was and took pity on me. He did not go through with the act. I should thank him because I'm sure it would not only have been painful (he was pretty big even by my more experienced standards!) but it showed his character as a sensitive, caring person. Most men would take advantage of such a situation. I did not feel very sexy or sensual at that moment in my life. Just silly, sophomoric and awkward. I can't say that I even had any expectations of how the sexual act would be for me. I never really thought of it as something ultra-special. I guess I saw it as more of a skill I needed to be familiar with in order to complete my femininity.

As I'm writing this, I realize how cold this must sound but you might have felt the same way about this subject if your parents never had a candid discussion with you about the opposite sex, let alone sex in general. My dad is a great guy, a real pal. He was never really too concerned about the personal matters of my sisters and I. Not even our academics. He left that to my mother. She was always the rock in our family. Every family has either a patriarch or a matriarch that rules the roost. In our family it was feminine energy all the way. My mother, for all her strength, could not foresee her own health problems. She had an aneurysm and a stroke when she was forty-five. I was fifteen at the time and I had more important things to worry about while I was in school besides dating and sex. Even when my romantic thoughts would occasionally creep in, I always squashed them.

I lost my virginity on my twenty-first birthday. I was working in the collections department of a bankcard corporation. One day a co-worker named Terri marched right up to me and chirped, "I know someone who likes you! You've got an admirer!" She told me his name was Paul, what he looked like and what department he worked in. She told me many nice things about him. He was a very intelligent man, cute, a musician and he was really interested in meeting me. I started noticing him because now all of a sudden, he was everywhere that I seemed to be in the building. He was okay-looking. He was a blue-eyed blonde, with curly-ish hair, looked about thirty, although he was actually twenty-six. Anyway, I noticed him but I didn't care too much. Terri approached me again about a week later and told me that Paul wanted to know if I wanted to meet him at a local bar for happy hour. At the time I was twenty years old and I knew I couldn't go to a bar, so I said that there was no way I could go. The following day he finally stopped me in my tracks. He cornered me before I got to the office and told me that he had had a crush on me for a very long time and could I please have dinner with him? Just so that you know, in all of my twenty years, I probably went on about three dates! I was so touched and flattered by his sweetness and obvious adoration of me that I accepted and I started dating him.

I got to know him so well. It's interesting that when you've never really explored the sexual side of your being how much you can be satisfied with just getting to know someone and not have the chemistry interfere, since it is not familiar to you yet. I loved talking to him. He was separated from his wife of four years and they had a two year old son together. His son was named after a character in a famous classic novel, so I won't say what it was but it made an impression on me. Paul was so intelligent and interesting to talk to. I was in heaven that a man like him could be so into me. He showered me with attention and in the short time we dated I absolutely felt like I was in love with him. The problem was that I was so repressed emotionally from having to squash my feelings for so long that I didn't know how to reciprocate the affection given to me. He was so fed up with what he considered my childish behavior that he broke up with me. I was devastated and heartbroken. I wanted him back and I wanted his love so badly!

My birthday was approaching and I wanted Paul to be with me. I called him and told him that for my birthday I wanted him to make love to me. At first he didn't want to because he knew I was a virgin. I had to talk him into it. I lied and told him I knew he didn't love me but it wasn't about being in love. I just needed to experience this sensuality, a dimension of my persona I had never experienced before. I appealed to his logic but I was lying the entire time. I really loved him! Also he didn't have to worry about birth control, since I had been on the pill since I was nineteen—although in this day and age, I would definitely make him wear a condom—but back in the 80s, it was a more naïve time.

The night before my big night I bought a teddy. I drove to his apartment and modeled the lingerie for him. I tried to be vampy but I allowed myself to be submissive with him. I let him tell me what to do. I allowed him to position me anyway he saw fit because the way I internalized it, he was the expert. Not only that but I truly wanted to please him. When he actually entered me, the vindictive side of me asked him, "Are you all the way inside me yet?" Of course he didn't miss a beat, he just plumbed deeper. The entire time I wanted to please him but I also wanted him to know that he didn't completely devastate me, so I moved my body the way I instinctively felt I should but I gave him no verbal feedback. I was hurting a bit physically and my leg muscles were sore. Afterwards, I just laid with him for awhile. He held me and was very sweet with me but I knew it wouldn't last. This wasn't love, at least not for him. I got dressed and got the hell out of there as soon as I could.

On my way home, I felt a sense of relief that I had accomplished my mission and at the time I had no regrets. In my mind, I was actually picking the act apart and discounting it quite a bit if I remember correctly. "Much ado about nothing" was my sentiment at the time. I carried these feelings over into the next day.

I heard from Paul the next morning. He was concerned and wanted to know how I felt about what had transpired between us. My only reply was to tell him, "It was nice but it didn't hurt as much as I thought it would." His voice changed when he retorted that there were other positions he could have used on me that would have had more impact. Well what could I say? I had to agree with him and I continued a sexual relationship with him for a couple more weeks. At least I had him to myself a little longer. However, I couldn't take it anymore. I still cared more about him than he did about me so I ended the affair.

Not even two weeks later he was dating someone else. Actually, he dated a few people at the same office building. It tore me apart but I put on a brave face and I never let him know how bad he made me feel. It took me almost two years to get over that experience. If I had to do my first sexual experience all over again, based on my family background, it would probably be more or less the same way. Unfortunately, my first sexual experience set a precedent for me. It confirmed what I believed sex to be all along—a skill I needed to employ in order to fully express my sensuality and femininity. Sex for many years was not truly a loving act but more recreational. It's not like I haven't had a good time with it. I do enjoy sex and I've had some good relationships. However, women are always the ones at a disadvantage for expressing and engaging in their sexuality. It seems as though men can do whatever they want with very little consequence to their character. Truthfully, even though I'm not a virgin anymore, I'm still waiting for my first real loving experience.

My parents didn't give me any advice. They never discussed sexual relationships at all.

Male: I'm 45. I was 24.

No, I really didn't have any expectations. I just wanted it to be as much fun for her as it was for me. She was a new girlfriend of mine who I had just recently met. We had gone out on three dates and were extremely hot and heavy on the first two and I sort of knew if I played my cards right the third date was going to be the lucky one.

My parents didn't give me any advice. They never discussed sexual relationships at all. As for advice from my friends, the one thing I remember was that when you did it you would most likely cum extremely fast (which I did) but that it was up to you and your partner to make sure you got it up again and did it a second time and make sure she was happy also. I did not receive any advice from religious figures at all—of course I never asked for it either.

We did it at her place in her bedroom. As I said earlier, I sort of thought it would happen the night it did so no, it did not take me by surprise at all.

She was on the Pill and that was all the protection we used.

As we were doing it I was both happy and thrilled. I was very gentle, as I was not too sure as to what I was doing. Having seen it in films and reading about it in magazines, I knew what you were supposed to do but having never done it, I wanted to make sure I was gentle with her and assure that she had a good time as well.

She was very happy when we were done—she had a great orgasm and after we were done I told her that she was my first. She was very pleased that I had chosen her. There was no problem getting it in, as she was as wet as I was hard.

The best part for me was cumming. Having never experienced it with a girl before, it was a thrilling moment. The worst part was having to pull out—it felt really good in there! Afterwards I felt great, as I had finally experienced what I had always wanted to and I think that she was as satisfied as I was. I felt great about her—she was very sexual, very pleasurable to me and wanted to make sure I was as happy as she was.

I never told anyone.

We're married—nineteen years this year.

I would have to say that there was chemistry there and that I knew she was the one that I wanted to do it with for the first time. Of course, her allowing me to do it also helped!

The experience didn't color my attitude towards sex. I enjoyed it then and still enjoy it today. It was a great experience and one that I still look back fondly on today.

Actually I would do it all the same again—she wore the perfect outfit (don't tell anyone but I love pantyhose and she wore them that night!)—did all the right things and it really was a great night.

I would tell virgins to make sure that the person you are going to do it with the first time is as happy and satisfied as you are. If you're going to do it, make sure you know that the person you're going to do it with is someone you can trust and continue to have a relationship with when you're done.

We *did it in a hotel. I was the aggressor and in my wildest, wildest, wildest dreams, I would never have thought that would be the case.*

Female: I am almost 44. I was 25 when I lost my virginity.

I wanted it to be with someone I felt I could trust and selfishly enough, I wanted it to be at a time when I did not feel embarrassed about being nude in front of a man. I wanted to feel attractive and I was waiting for a magical time when I would have it like I had seen on TV and read about in books—that thing called libido or sex-drive.

I had never watched porn nor had I barely ever seen a man. I was painfully shy and ashamed of my body, so I never really got close to someone. I didn't know, or even begin to know, what to expect.

He was a production assistant on a mini-series. We were often working on the set together (I was a stand-in and he was on the set most of the time.) He was (I think) twenty-four or twenty-five. I had known him for about five months.

I was out of town when it happened and I didn't tell anyone until at least ten years later.

My parents, of course, wanted me to wait. What I heard from my friends was that it was greater than sliced bread. It was between that and don't even look at a guy because all he wants is…. All of this from the general populace, not anyone in particular.

Religious advice was that thinking it was the same as doing it (Catholic, in case you don't recognize it). Don't use birth control because that is a sin. Oh and don't do it out of wedlock. Oh and do it only with your spouse, not your cousins (skip that last thing) or maybe not.

We did it in a hotel. I was the aggressor and in my wildest, wildest, wildest dreams, I would never have thought that would be the case.

The birth control situation: okay, this was soooooo funny. I got a sponge from the other stand-in. She told me what to do but she failed to tell me about the part where you could put your finger right through it, especially if you just happen to have a pretty decent set of nails growing. So, yes that's what happened and I used faulty logic—and I say again for any virgin who may be reading this at this moment—faulty, faulty, faulty logic that I would not be in ovulation because my schedule had been knocked out of whack by rapid weight loss and change of life style and the observation that my last period was all of about three drops. On the minor chance that you are wondering if I got pregnant—no. I was extremely lucky. My period was off schedule and when my period was late, I was fumbling around with (brand new on the market) an early pregnancy kit at the drug store wondering who I could ask about how early in a pregnancy did these kits work. Very sobering.

I had just dumped a bunch of weight and felt more attractive than I had in my entire life. That, coupled with the fact that I really was attracted to the guy and he was sweet and smart (and I thought liked me too), made for a hormonal flood of me-woman-him-man. I experienced a kind of rush of emotion and desire for him AND I thought this was my only shot at finding out what IT was all about. (Strange visiting my twenty-five year old self after so many years. How different we both think!)

As far as the act itself: Did it hurt? A shocked, resounding YES (which, I might add, would be one big point for the make sure you love and trust each other argument).

I was happy, scared and sad all at the same time. It's so strange how one person can experience such a wide range of emotions in such a short time. Yes, it was pretty short, all of about three minutes, which when I think of it, seemed pretty long at the time. At first came the scared part, which was mixed with the happy part. Scared because I didn't know what I was doing (performance anxiety) but happy that he was going to do it with me and when it was done I was embarrassed and sad that I would always remember my first time as stupid and awkward. Now I just laugh at the two puppies who didn't know what the hell they were doing.

He was very respectful and as I recall, quiet. He did have a bit of a hard time getting his penis inside.

The best part was the talking and kissing before, believing he wanted me as much as I wanted him and feeling attractive and like I was finally getting to grow up and feel what a real woman was supposed to, whatever that meant

Okay, now it's funny but then it definitely defined the worst moment, just about in my whole life, when he announced that he was going to cum. I had an epiphany, a grounding as it were, a moment of sheer reality. I panicked and said, "Oh you better not. I didn't use anything!" Without a sound he rolled off (I'm having a truly gut rocking laugh at this moment blended with the slightest twinge of that old groan of regretful embarrassment) and to this day I don't know for sure if he did cum that night, in me or out of me. We both laid there without a word. I slept off and on after laying there for hours wishing that, by some miracle, I had just experienced a bad dream or that I could turn back the hands of time just this once.

Afterward, I felt regret. I realized that he was as inexperienced as me.

The only person I told was the stand-in who gave me the sponge.

He went back to good old Santa Monica and I went back to good old Charleston South Carolina. I asked him to send me his picture and after I sent him a nice bunch of photos taken by the still photographer on the project, he sent me a letter and his headshot. I still have it but I very, very rarely look at it. I have been tempted to throw it out but that was a chapter of my life and there it stays.

The reason I chose to lose my virginity with him, at that time, was I didn't think I would have another opportunity to find out what all the fuss was about and I did really like him. If I saw him again, we would (if he has matured like a normal man) probably laugh mercilessly and talk about what we remember about the whole thing.

The experience didn't color my attitude toward sex. I was such a pup for my age but even then I realized that it takes two and it is probably best if at least one knows what they are doing. I later met my first husband who was a lot more experienced and would respectfully and with fun show me what he liked and was very knowledgeable and generous, so no great lasting effect.

Looking back, I recall two people trying to fumble their way through their first sexual encounter. If I had it to do again I definitely would not have done it, for many reasons. It did nothing for me nor did it for him and I have reason to believe that word got around to the crew and they got a very wrong impression about me, which is never a good thing.

There really is no rush to have your first experience. For me, it felt like I would never have sex if I didn't do it right then. I now know that I was allowing external factors and cues (TV, magazines, other people's stories, musical lyrics, etc.) push me into thinking that I had to know what it was all about. I also allowed those cues to convince me that I was not a well adjusted, emotionally mature woman unless I knew what sex was like (in fact could perform

like a hooker) and wanted it every day. Sex can be really great with a man that you love and that you know in your heart of hearts loves you but it is like anything else. Some people like to do it more and some like to do it less. Some people like to read, some like to run, paint, sing, etc. Go at your own pace. It is like that saying about love. You know it when you know it. If you let that part happen first (the love), your first time will be better than if you don't. More than likely it won't be your all to end all. It may be awkward but instead of feeling embarrassed, you will have something to snicker about when you're old and gray.

When guys are horny, they'll think with the head in their pants rather than the one on their shoulders.

Male: I am 32 years old and I lost my virginity when I was 27 years old.

The first time I had sex, it was pretty much like I thought it would be—warm, wet and felt great! It was much better than masturbating. My first time wound up being with the woman that I eventually married a year and half later. My job sent me to a large pharmaceutical company to work for three months. Marta, a gorgeous thirty-five year old who worked in the group where I was placed, volunteered to show me around the area since I didn't know where anything was. I was definitely attracted to her and was ecstatic that she wanted show me around. We started dating and had sex for the first time after we had dated for about a month and a half.

I was raised in a Catholic home with two great parents. My mom had said that sex is for when you are married and in a committed relationship. I don't think she was naïve enough to think that my brothers followed this advice but I was always the obedient one and at the time felt that she was right. My dad would say the same things but when I got older in high school he said that he was once my age and he knew guys had sex with girls and that if I did I had to use a condom so as not to get the girl pregnant. Not much was said about STDs or anything of the like by either of them.

When I was in high school, I dated a girl that went to the all-girl school across town (I went to the all-boys high school). I knew that she wanted to have sex but I was really nervous and always put it off. I told a couple of my guy friends this and surprisingly, they were all really cool about it. Jack, a good friend who had been having sex for about two years, told me that while it felt great, it was not all that it was hyped-up to be. He was always worrying that his girlfriend would get pregnant and that if I didn't feel comfortable, I should stick to my guns. I guess I was also a little shy and worried that maybe my penis wasn't big enough, or I would not know what to do, or that she would get pregnant; typical things that a seventeen or eighteen year old may feel.

The high school I attended was run by Catholic priests. During my junior and senior years, the Lifestyles class was taught by a married Greek Orthodox priest. He was very cool and definitely wanted the guys to be comfortable asking questions. If someone would make a joke or laugh when talking about sex, he was very good at turning the tables and making the guy red with embarrassment. While he taught the same thing about having sex and being able to handle the consequences (which no seventeen or eighteen year old can), he readily acknowledged guys in class would have sex and taught us about the different methods of birth control. Growing up, my mom was a nurse and would speak very frankly with us, so I knew quite a bit going into the class. I was always cognizant of the fact that pregnancy could occur even with birth control, so that furthered me not wanting to jump into anything.

My first time having sex was in a rental condo that the company put me up in for the couple of months I was working. Marta and I would play around in bed and do everything except have sex. I remember making out one night until 2 am and not having sex. She was PISSED!!! She really wanted to get laid. I did too but I didn't have any condoms and she wasn't on any birth control. She kept telling me that she couldn't get pregnant since she had some medical condition and didn't really ovulate (although she had a period). I stuck firm and we just rolled over and went to sleep. The next day I stopped at the drugstore and bought a box of non-lubricated condoms, as she said that she was sensitive to the lubricant. Two nights later she stayed over and we were fooling around and she asked if I had gotten the condoms to which I replied, "Here they are!" So, I guess I knew that I was going to have sex (even though I wasn't married!) but didn't know exactly when.

Since I was not very experienced (she didn't know this but I think suspected it—I told her that I had been with one other girl back where I lived. Not true but I did have some romantic involvement with a girl, we just had not had sex), I told her that I wanted her on top of me. I didn't want to feel awkward about trying to find the right angle or missing the opening completely. She readily obliged and then slid down me very slowly, sighing loudly while she was doing it. As I said earlier, it felt warm, wet and awesome. I remember thinking "Oh my God, I'm having sex and it feels awesome." The feeling was one that I had never experienced when masturbating. Having a person on top you that is moving and moaning because of you is a little overwhelming. She asked me to slap her ass which made her moan more and made me feel like a rock star! I only lasted about three minutes before I climaxed. She was very happy and asked me if I liked it. I just held her and said that it was awesome. As we went to sleep, I laid there thinking "I'm no longer a virgin" and you know, I didn't feel bad about it. Catholic guilt can be very strong and surprisingly, I didn't feel much of it. There was maybe a little part of me that felt I let myself down, as I really thought I would wait 'til I was married to have sex.

Having sex with her made me feel closer to her. When we had sex, I knew that I was falling hard for her. She had come out of a bad relationship about eight months before we met and kept telling me that she was damaged and I should find someone else. I have always been a pleaser and want to help people feel better. So I think that I stuck around because I knew she felt better when she was with me (and I felt happy when I was with her). After we had sex for the first time, it really made me feel close and connected with her.

I didn't tell anyone about it at first. I had a good friend back in Southern California who I called about two weeks after our first time to tell him that Marta was awesome and also to brag that we had sex that afternoon and she climaxed four times and then called me on her way home to thank me. As a guy, that made me feel like a total stud and I had to share it with a buddy. He gave the appropriate kudos and asked if I was falling in love with her. I told him that I thought I might be falling for her.

Marta and I continued to date and grow closer and about a year and half after having sex for the first time, we got married. We've now been married for about five years. I chose to lose my virginity to Marta because as an adult, I felt that it was time for me to do it. She was actually interested in me.

I have to say, though, that from about the time I was about eighteen until I was twenty-three I was about seventy-five pounds overweight. At my max, I weighed about two hundred eighty-five and felt that no girl would ever want to be with someone who was this heavy. I made a decision to lose weight, not just because I wanted an attractive girlfriend but I also had developed high blood pressure. After losing the weight, I noticed that when I went out with friends, girls were taking much more interest in me. But I always wondered if they would have been attracted to me when I was heavy and that was an emotional killer for me. I didn't pursue many women even though I had lost a lot of weight. Marta was different to me. I told her about my weight loss when we first dated. After she got to know me, she was honest and said that if I was still really heavy, she probably would not have dated me. She said that since knowing me and seeing that I had a nice personality and was very caring, she would have missed out on something if I was heavier and she chose not go out with me. After being married, she said that she could care less now if I gained weight but says that she knows I wouldn't be happy if I got heavy again. She's right and the weight has stayed off for about seven years.

Losing my virginity to her was the best thing that I could have done because she cared for me. I didn't give in to her pressure to have sex until about two weeks after we started becoming intimate. She accepted this (and I'm sure she thought it was weird—a guy turning down sex). We did a lot of foreplay during that time, which was great and I think that helped me to get over some of my anxiety about being a virgin. I was able to become more familiar with her anatomy and what made her feel good, which in turn boosted my confidence. I was going down on her before we had sex and when she climaxed, she said that I was the first guy she had been with that was able to make her climax orally. She had been with about six other guys up until that time. Talk about an ego booster. Here I am, a virgin and she's asking who taught me to please a women that way. I guess watching a porno has some advantages!

Having sex for the first time didn't really change my attitude towards sex. I know that most people have sex earlier than I did and if you are a player, you don't care how you get your rocks off. Since I'm not like that, I guess maybe I still felt that sex was something that happens AND means something when you are with someone you care about. I know, probably a little naïve on my part but it's what I feel.

I sometimes think back to the first time when I masturbate, even today. I relive the experience, feelings and sensations that I felt the first time. I think I'm able to do it since I only lost my virginity about seven years ago. I still feel that it was one of the most special and memorable times of my life and one that I won't ever forget. Sometimes I think I'm trying to re-capture that feeling of wild abandon when I have sex with my wife. There's not much about the experience of losing my virginity that I would change. Maybe if I was more confident, that would have made the experience better. But losing my virginity to someone who had a lot more experience than me made the situation a lot easier.

Advice I would give to virgins today. When guys are horny, they'll think with the head in their pants rather than the one on their shoulders.

Having sex the first time is very emotional. I think I was better able to appreciate that when I was older than if I had had sex when I was younger. A lot of guys who I knew in high school who had sex were very cavalier about their girlfriends and today, they are still the same way. Since I don't know how a girl feels that is still a virgin, I can only surmise that they may feel some of the same things. With the statistics showing the number of STDs that are transmitted even with oral sex, I think someone needs to think long and hard before having sex the first time. If your virginity means something to you, you have to be the stronger person and realize that if someone pressures you to have sex and you don't feel comfortable, that person will most likely treat you like crap afterwards. Trust me, I've seen it happen with my own two eyes.

I lost my virginity in the back seat of a 57 Chevy convertible...

Female: I am 59. I was 18.

I had no expectations about sex, no clues, it was the furthest thing from my mind.

He was my very first fiancé. He was twenty-one. I knew him from the time I was twelve and we had been dating about a year.

Advice from parents? Hell no! Sex was a four letter word. Noooo. None. I was always told not to do it until I was married. As far as the sex stuff is concerned, it was never discussed.

I lost my virginity in the back seat of a 57 Chevy convertible after a party.

It was a surprise. I never dreamed I'd do anything like that. I didn't use birth control, didn't even know about it.

I was scared, I felt ashamed. I felt I was going to hell. What's he gonna think of me tomorrow???? God, if I get pregnant!! It was not a pleasant experience.

I remember it being very uncomfortable. I don't remember it being a pleasant thing at all. Never made me feel like I wanted to do it again. I think he was as naïve as I was and I think we were both very clumsy.

I guess the worst part was feeling ashamed. The best part is—to be honest, I don't think there was a best part the first time. I really don't. I just felt ashamed. I felt like Oh my God, wait 'till I tell Nicole (my best friend).

I still absolutely do know him. We dated for a long time. We were planning to get married and then I met my first husband and pushed him aside (laughs). And I do still know him. I see him from time to time, I run into him.

My attitude toward sex hadn't really been colored but I think it made it easier the second time.

Looking back, I don't have that same feeling like it was a shameful thing. I think that it wasn't all that bad that I did what I did. I mean I really felt like I was in love, I really felt like he was the man I was going to marry.

Is that a good enough answer?

I had the full range of emotions all in one thirty-minute trip. I was scared, excited, confused and everything. The one emotion that I never experienced was confidence.

Male: I am 31 years old. The first time that I had sex was when I was 18.

Up to that point I had had only two girlfriends. My closest experience to sex was touching a girl's boobs. I had seen porn and engaged in masturbation but no sex. The girl who I first had sex with was a girl named Maria. She came around the dorm when I was in college. She was interested in one of my friends, so I had seen her around a couple times. I believe she was seventeen. The truth is I didn't know her. I may have said a couple things to her in passing. She was in the dorm off and on, not really there to see me.

I never had the opportunity to get advice from my mother. So my dad provided all the "talks" with me. Actually it was just one talk. My father sat my brother and me down after my sister had her first child. She was only fifteen. He said to us, "If you're going to have sex you better protect

> ### Sex on television can't hurt you unless you fall off.
> *Woody Allen (maybe)*
> *Source: en.wikiquote.org/wiki/Television*

yourself, because if you get her pregnant then you're going to be a father and your whole life will be out of your control." Let me remind you that I was thirteen and never even considered having a girlfriend at that point. So, this whole speech didn't make sense to me but it scared the hell out of me.

No one really talked to me about it. I didn't express my interests in sex to my friends because I didn't want them to pressure me into sleeping with just anyone. I kind of knew that when it was going to happen I would know it and just go for it. So there was no pressure and I chose the right situation for me to experience sex for the first time.

All my life I grew up in the church. I knew that sex was something that was emotionally uplifting and that it was special. I didn't ever think that I would hold out for marriage but I wanted it to be on my terms. I was never scared into thinking that sex was a bad thing but actually learned that sex was a great thing to be shared with someone special.

The first time that I had sex was in an empty dorm room on a vacant floor of our dorm. I have to admit that this was a not a surprise for me. The story goes like this. Charlie was actually dating someone at the time. He hung out with Maria but didn't want to lose his girlfriend. So one weekend when his girlfriend came into town he asked me to distract Maria for him. Maria knew about Susan but Susan didn't know about Maria. So, being his good friend, I stepped in to help. Maria came to the dorm like the normal weekend and I met her there. I introduced myself to her as her boyfriend and said that Susan was in town and we needed to be an attractive couple. How that worked I couldn't tell you but hey, it did. We introduced ourselves to Susan and went to the party as couples. As the night went on, I noticed that Maria was starting to pay attention to me instead of Charlie, so I returned the favor. The great thing was neither of us drank, so I can't blame it on alcohol. We just danced and kissed all night until I said to her I couldn't take it anymore. I told her that I wanted to be alone with her. So we went to my room and things started heating up. I had a pretty selfish roommate at the time. So I took her to the vacant part of the dorm. To my surprise one of the rooms happened to be unlocked. We took advantage of the space and she tore me up.

I did use a condom. I was so scared that I didn't even consider not using protection. I was given some condoms at the freshman orientation as a gag gift from my senior pal.

When we started having sex I was shaking scared and she could tell. I told her that I had never had sex before and she said it was fine. I think she enjoyed being in control anyway. So, being the rookie and ready to please, I said, "You tell me what to do and I'll do it." She told me to lie on my back and she would do the rest. So I laid down and she did the work. She put the condom on after a few minutes of oral pleasure and then climbed on top. I couldn't help myself but to put my hands all over her huge breasts. I think this helped me out because I was so focused on them that I didn't concentrate on my penis. She was riding me and breathing heavy and moaning and then it turned into a sweaty groan. I was so taken back by her groaning that I lost it and came as hard as I could. Sweat everywhere. I looked at the clock and it had been only twenty minutes. I didn't know if that was good or bad so I told her I wasn't done. I actually took the condom off, cleaned myself and we did the whole thing over. She gave me oral pleasure until I was hard again and then climbed on top. This time I was focused on her action and didn't last very long at all. I had the full range of emotions all in one thirty-minute trip. I was scared, excited, confused and everything. The one emotion that I never experienced was confidence. Even when I wanted to try to please her a second time, I did it out of fear of not pleasing her the first time.

I was really trying to make her feel good about having sex with someone she didn't know. I was gentle with her until she told me what to do. I was definitely awkward because this was the first time and I didn't know when or where to touch. I was really clueless. Sex is definitely not porn. I didn't really say anything to her except that she was awesome. She was so into it I felt like I would kill the mood by saying something stupid.

I think that she was pretty excited. I know that when I said we were not done her eyes opened up quite a bit and she couldn't quit smiling. When we finished the second round she just laid on my chest for quite a while. Then at some point in the night she said she had to go home.

I didn't have any trouble getting it in. I wouldn't say that I am big at all. I am average or just above average in size. She had sex before, so she knew what she was doing and I just let her go for it.

The best part of the experience was definitely watching her being pleased. When she was riding me and sweat was flowing everywhere, I felt pretty excited myself. The worst part was when we were getting started and I didn't know what I was doing. I felt so confused and scared. I didn't know what to say or do. I am so glad she was comfortable and took over.

The best way to describe my feelings is I was happy. I was excited about the fact that I had finally had sex. I did it with a very attractive young woman. I wasn't so bad that she just got off of me and left right afterwards. On the other hand, I didn't know how to react to the fact that this was a one-time thing. We never avoided each other and we even made reference to it but I always wondered was it going to end as being a one-night fling. And the answer to date is yes; it ended as a one-night fling.

My feelings about her never really changed. She was there and we would chat at times. Even though things with her and Charlie never got going because he was with Susan, we never seemed interested enough in each other to try and date or anything.

I did tell people about it but it took awhile. I wasn't one to go around and pat myself on the back for anything, especially that. It was a moment that Maria and I shared and it was great. So I wanted to keep it that way. Later I told my best friend and my brothers.

I have no idea what became of her. This was at the end of my freshman year in college. I saw her a couple more times at the dorm but nothing after that semester. I couldn't even ask Charlie because he transferred schools to be closer to Susan.

I lost my virginity with that girl at that time because I just felt that I was ready in my life to take on the experience of sex. I was in a situation where I was spending the evening with an attractive girl. We were sharing a wonderful moment and I didn't want to lose my chance. I didn't know if or when that opportunity would come around again.

I believe that the experience reinforced my attitudes towards sex. I understand why people engage in sexual activities but people misuse it or abuse it. I still today feel that sex is an experience that two people need to share together. It doesn't have to be a marriage or a long-term relationship but I won't have sex with a stranger again.

I wouldn't change a thing. I think that the first experience needs to be just that, the first experience. It doesn't have to be right or correct or even good. All those things are nice but not necessary. Like anything else, you learn through experience. With that being said, don't go out and have sex with just anyone just to increase your experiences. As for virgins, take pride in your virginity. Sex is a wonderful experience that needs to be shared with someone wonderful. If you are holding out for marriage or the right situation, then hold out. Don't be with a person based on sex alone. It is the shortest time spent in a relationship. Attitude, communication and respect are far more important factors than sex.

My mother had told me about the 1950s. There were good girls who wore Bermudas and got married and there were biker female Brandos who spit gravel and got laid.

Female: I'm 47 years old. I'm not certain how old I was.

Most people are raised. I simply wasn't. I was a free range chicken that just happened to have two parents, a bedroom and an environment that was called home. My coming of age was a paradox: the more parental guidance I needed, the less they dealt with me. When I first got my period, while unfortunately wearing white hip-hugger jeans with a nasty yet trendy strawberry patch on the knee, I was practicing the refined art of being a juvenile delinquent. I really never was one but I had to have something to do. The other option was to stay at home, where orthopedic shoes and kilts reigned and where I was obliged to survive the infantile mood swings of my under-trust-funded adult child parent and his enabler, my martyrized mother. He would fly off the handle and we would be lined up in submission to hear about the BILLS. But anyway you want to know about my hymen, not my cerebellum.

Back to my period. There I was hanging outside a suburban McDonald's. I called my mother from a pay phone and asked what to do. She directed me to the nearest drugstore where I was to buy a box of super Tampax and a jar of Vaseline. That was the extent of the mother-daughter dialogue.

My mother had told me about the 1950s. There were good girls who wore Bermudas and got married and there were biker female Brandos who spit gravel and got laid. My mother got married because she was afraid to break loose and her legacy to me has been a series of very subtly ingrained ideas that will stay with me for the duration of my time on the planet. Marriage being a no-no is one of them. But luckily my options were a bit more varied, it wasn't so black and white.

It was the seventies and the whole western world was screwing each other in a big frenzy of unprotected sex. *TV Guide* had warnings on its cover. There were TV shows showing parents how to recognize if their kids were smoking reefers. I may have been only in eighth grade but I quickly figured out that, since I was already stuck in the suburbs, my direction had better be out. And out for good. Furthermore, I had all these references available to me. *TV Guide* said sunglasses and sloppy long hair, wrecked blue jeans, military anti-war gear and other such paraphernalia were symptomatic of being a druggie. I did what any adolescent with spirit would do, I went for it. But I added the Lolita touch, wearing head scarves as halter tops with hip-huggers, gold chain linked shoes and Jackie O glasses. I looked like trailer trash come to town. I am slowly making my way to my first sexual experience. But the build-up is that I was a total, full-scale, head-on temptation and was totally unaware of it. I can't even believe my parents would let me out of the house.

Time passed and I left junior high and graduated to high school. This had a lot of consequences. Quaaludes were available in the hallways, half the students were on LSD and a few of the teachers too. By this time I was already calming down some. I developed a crush on an older guy who I met at a college mixer dance but unfortunately he had a girlfriend. So I was fifteen and I think they were either nineteen or twenty. I was kind of like their mascot. They both knew I had a huge crush on him and I guess they thought it was cute.

We were all part of a gang. We went on camping trips, to concerts, we all spent lots of time in different people's parents' basements. Everybody was getting laid but me. One night, Lynn, she was the girlfriend, died in a car accident on her way home from an Eric Clapton concert. I inherited a boyfriend.

I knew what it meant. I knew he would have expectations sexually of me. So the next morning I went to Roy Rogers and sat down and ate six roast beef sandwiches with BBQ sauce to overcome my grief and fear. What was worse is that I really loved Lynn and it was a loss for me in spite of the gain of a boyfriend. I think I was fifteen but losing my virginity means nothing to me. As far as I am concerned it was just another day in my life. To be frank, I could have been fourteen, or fifteen, or sixteen. I am not really sure.

Anyway I went over to this guy's basement, where he was crying and it was all too emotional. He wanted to have sex but I was too freaked out. So he gave me a couple of downers and we did it. I think it was boring. Then he walked me home and I was afraid he would never talk to me again. So he sat on my parents' porch all night drinking beer and tossing the cans in the yard and when I woke up for school he was there and he said, "I still like you." My father threw a shit fit about the beer cans.

He was an alright person. An awful lay with a miniscule penis but that is another story unto itself. It took me until the following year to discover that all sex is not the same. I went to the biggest stud in the neighborhood's house. I think he was twenty-six and I told him I wanted to learn about sex. I was such a wild child that it makes me laugh to think about it.

My advice is never let anyone pressure you into sex and if they do, get over it. Sex is wonderful, sex is great. It can also get really boring because sex is usually accompanied by bother.

I felt friendship and love for him and it ended with a feeling of betrayal.

Male: I am 48. I was 12 when I had my first homosexual experience. I was 19 when I had my first experience with a woman.

As far as expectations go, I thought it would be magical and certainly wanted that feeling. The boy was my friend. We attended the same school and I had known him for eight years. He was also twelve.

I knew I was gay, or at least bi, when I was twelve. The only advice I got from my parents was to be careful and avoid getting a girl pregnant. They figured that school would take care of educating me about the rest. Nothing at all from my friends. I was schooled by Catholic nuns and priests and their only advice was ABSTINENCE.

My friend and I did it on my brother's bed. I planned it with him. Basically, I seduced him while we were looking at porn magazines. We didn't use protection. This was way before AIDS.

I thought it was so cool to play with my best friend and to see his penis and his body and that we were having fun together. It was really intimate and fun. I was happy during the sex, scared when I came and then sad when we never really talked again. I was very gentle and sweet but I know I was also awkward. I felt that we were having fun and wanted more. But then he never wanted to play again.

The best part was the intimacy but the worst part was losing my friend. I had a great time before, during and after but then later on that week I thought, "Shit! Where's my friend?" I felt friendship and love for him and it ended with a feeling of betrayal.

I didn't tell anyone about it afterwards.

He's since gone through two or three wives and I don't know what happened after that. We lost touch.

I chose to lose my virginity with him because he was my friend, we liked the same things and we were having a great time together. It seemed like the logical next step.

As far as coloring my attitude towards sex, that experience taught me not to express interest in guys for a long time—many years.

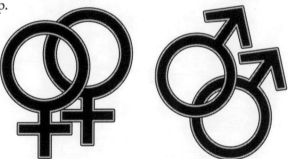

Now that I'm older and look back on it, I wish that I had known how to talk to him. If I could go back in time, I'd do more to pleasure him, to make sure that he enjoyed himself so much that he wanted more. I missed him tremendously.

My advice to virgins is not to feel pressured in any way to have sex or to save your virginity. Just be sure what you are doing is what you want and be ready to accept the consequences. Life is too short not to do what is best for you. Keep your eyes and mind open. Change what you can and accept what you cannot.

Editor's note: Regarding the woman, all the respondent said was that she was thirty and was a woman he worked with. He felt that he'd been gentle, sweet and awkward with her as well, had no problem getting inside of her and that she was on the pill. He wrote that if the right situation came along, he'd sleep with a woman again.

I *could hear guys outside the door listening. They sounded amused. I am sure they were titillated. Did Jonah tell them of his plans?*

Female: 37 years old. I was 17.

It took me to the eleventh grade before I figured out that there were "bad crowds" at my high school. Actually, they were more naughty than bad. There were pothead vocational students, all the way up to the recreational drinkers and pill poppers from the football team and cheerleader squad. They all drank a little too much beer on the weekends and did a little too much coke during the week. It was all very discreet and somewhat intriguing to the likes of me because there was always a hint of sex behind it all. It was just a hint but it hung in the air over the very halls I walked.

I was a good girl up until my senior year. I did my own thing, which didn't include drinking, partying or sex. I wanted to go to college. I had the intelligence and the grades to go to college. I took most of the necessary high school college courses. I even dressed the part—plaid skirts with the big safety pins, Izod sweaters, Docksiders and argyle socks. My electives were all art related: media, journalism, drama, string ensemble and yearbook staff.

I held a B average. I was the poster girl for innocence and purity. I was a good girl but something was missing and it wasn't until early spring of 1984 that I discovered what it was.

His name was Jonah. He was a junior and a vocational student. We met by chance through a mutual friend while working on the set of the spring musical. We didn't travel the same halls or circles. We didn't like the same type of music. In fact we had very little in common. But I was sure of one thing. He was a bad boy. He smoked. He drank. He always had pot on him. He wore a black leather jacket. And I was sure he had had sex before. I thought I could tell just by looking at him. And looking back on it, I could not have been more right. He was every father's worst nightmare and he was exactly what I wanted. It wasn't long before we were going out.

We made a very odd couple and it wasn't long before everyone had something to say about it. My parents were not thrilled. My friends couldn't figure out why I was going out with him. His friends felt the same. But I didn't care, nor did I listen. I was having far too much fun crossing over to the bad side. He got me stoned. We went to parties together. I started smoking. But best of all, he wanted me. We made out all of the time and gave each other hickies. We fondled each other over clothes and under clothes. He made me crazy and I wanted him so bad. The strange thing, though, is that I couldn't bring myself to say yes to going all the way. We came close a few times but when the moment of truth came I said no. I could see the disappointment in his face but he never pressured me or made me feel bad about it or myself.

What was I afraid of? I had many ideas and thoughts and opinions about sex. I knew that some of my friends were having it and seemed to like it. I knew basically how it was done, thanks to biology and health classes and the lovely little book about puberty that my parents handed to me in silence, hoping it was the answer to all of my questions. I knew I wasn't going to be an expert at it the first time out, which was a relief and I knew it was going to hurt, which wasn't. I had no real expectations, or any idea, of what it would be like or how it should be. I had not seen much on television (TV had not progressed to that point yet) and I rarely saw an R rated movie. What little information I got from my parents revolved around waiting until I was in love and married and always use birth control. AIDS was still a gay disease and was not considered an epidemic, so it was not an issue for me. But one issue I did have to deal with was location. I lived with my parents and had no car. The same went for him. Was my first time going to be a quickie in the woods or in some friend's basement? I knew

> *Desperate is not a sexual preference.*
> *- Randy K. Milholland, Something Postive, 01-08-09*
> *Source: www.quotationspage.com*

I didn't like the sound of that. I did want it to be sweet and romantic and not rushed and in the back of my mind I didn't want to stress out about it anymore. I wanted it to be over with. I didn't have to wait much longer.

It was Friday the 13th, 1984. It was exactly fifty-eight days away from my eighteenth birthday and my high school graduation. Rumor had it that one of my classmates had access to his cousin's apartment for a few days and was going to have a toga party. The rumor turned out to be true. When I got home from school that afternoon I asked my mother if I could attend my girlfriend Tina's sleepover party. I got permission and a ride. I should have been feeling guilty for lying but I was too excited thinking about being with Jonah all night long.

After I was dropped off at Tina's I walked on over to Jonah's. His parents were still at work, so we smoked out in his room. We had plans to meet some of the partygoers at the local theater to see an early showing of *Friday the 13th*. One of Jonah's friends was going to pick us up for the movie and then drop us off at the party. I was so excited. I had a buzz going, Jonah and I had made out a little already, the movie was going to be totally scary and then we were going to a "real" party afterwards, without any supervision and hang out all night long. In all of my seventeen years, three hundred eight days and nineteen hours of life I don't think I had ever felt so free and alive.

By ten o'clock the movie was over and we were in a car heading towards the party. A light spring rain was falling and we were still a little high from smoking and a little crazed from the movie. The party was in full swing when we got there. We didn't have a toga but it seemed everyone else did. The music was blaring and the togas were dancing and drinking. We joined right in. Now, up until this point in my life I had never been drunk. Sure I had the occasional two beers at a party or a stolen glass of Champagne at Christmas but never rip roaring, three sheets to the wind, fall down laughing kind of drunk. There was so much alcohol at this party I could have taken a bath in it. And it was free. The guys at the party seemed extra willing to fetch you more whenever your cup ran dry. Jonah seemed especially willing to refill mine. If there was an ulterior motive on his part, I didn't see it. I was having a blast. And so was everyone else, guys and girls alike.

A little after midnight, Jonah and I realized we were out of cigarettes. We decided to take a little break from the festivities and walk in the rain the two blocks to the all night convenience store. We laughed and stumbled and kissed our way there and back. I just kept thinking what a great night I was having, a night I would never forget. I could not have been more right.

When we got back to the party it was in full force but all of the girls were gone. It was late after all and apparently I was the only one who lied to her parents so she could stay out all night. Jonah and I were both soaked from our walk (was that part of his plan?) so he led me into the bathroom to get dried off. My inhibitions were pretty much gone, so I just took off most of my wet clothes and started wringing them over the sink. The next five or ten minutes (it seemed no time at all) are still a little blurry in my mind. I think that's because I still cannot believe that he got me to lie down on the bathroom floor. I can understand why he wanted to—I was his naked, wet, drunk, virginal girlfriend. I cannot blame him. I do remember feeling him press up behind me at the sink and then taking off my bra. When I turned around he was naked and hard. He kissed me and kept on kissing me. He must have pulled us both to the floor because the next thing I knew he was on top of me and pulling my panties down. I think at first I liked it. I had let him get almost this far in the past. But once again fear set in. Birth control should have entered my mind but it didn't. This time I think the fear was more about what people would think. I could hear guys outside the door listening. They sounded amused. I am sure they were titillated. Did Jonah tell them of his plans? To this day I have no idea. In any case I know I told Jonah no. It was obviously not the right time or place for me. But it was for him. I tried to argue with him. I told him I wanted him but this was a stranger's bathroom floor. I could think of a thousand better places and a thousand better circumstances. If I had not been drunk I believe I could have stopped him again.

It did not take him very long to penetrate. I know I offered a bit of resistance but he was of average size and apparently knew what he was doing. It hurt but not as bad as I expected it to. I felt no physical pleasure during the act. Mentally my mind was racing. I had done it. It was over. Thank God it was over. Now I could offer myself to him freely because the deed was done. The rest of the night was insane. I drank more. We had sex again but this time on a bed in what I gathered was the apartment owner's bedroom. I enjoyed it more the second time. The mystery was gone. I was relieved. I felt like I could regain control of the sex situation.

Afterwards I drank even more. I was losing control of the reality situation. By 4:00 am I was completely and utterly drunk. I remember only scary highlights of the night. I was jumping up and down on the bed naked. I lost my gold necklace with the "84' charm on it. Everyone had passed out. The host was pissed off at me because I had been cavorting around the place topless for an hour and told me he knew what had happened in the bathroom. He pointed out that my boyfriend had passed out. He pointed to the bloodstain on my panties and shook his head. He said that he had kept the other guys from taking advantage of me that night because Jonah didn't seem to care one way or the other. I got pissed off and told him I was going outside to go jump in front of a car. (I was really, really drunk by this point.) I tried to leave but he held me back. I woke up on the couch with a blanket over me.

That morning I had play practice at the high school across the street. A few of the guy's girlfriends had dropped in to pick them up or to see them and were surprised to see me still there. I felt a bit embarrassed but thank God I managed to dress myself beforehand. At rehearsal I told my best friend Dawn what had happened and she seemed happy for me. I think perhaps I might have obsessed too much over it with her. She had her first experience three years before me. I didn't tell anyone else for a long time.

In the days following, Jonah and I had sex probably a dozen more times. We had it after my senior prom and after his junior prom. I had introduced him to my friend Wayne at my senior prom and a few days short of my graduating high school Jonah and Wayne insisted that I get together with them and their friend Shelly at Shelly's house. Little did I know that Wayne and Shelly were gay and that the hope was that they, Jonah and Wayne, could pass me off onto her while they got together. I had no clue.

I was kissing Jonah when Wayne walked in and he got very upset and ran out the back door. Jonah left me and ran after him. Shelly tried to "console" me. I threw Jonah's class ring on the counter and left. I was pissed. I really liked Jonah a lot. But I also had the feeling that things would have never moved past where they were and I did not want to be with a bisexual. Jonah had served his purpose. And he had also released a sexual dervish.

I never blamed Jonah for who he was or for choosing Wayne over me. I had no time to. I moved quickly into several different sexual relationships. I wanted more and more experience. But at the same time I never lost sight of my real goal, which was a true love and a lasting relationship. I probably lost a few good guys because I slept with them too fast. But I probably lost a few bad ones as well. I think for a while I used sex to attract men instead of using my personality and my intelligence. I blame that mostly on youth.

When I look back on the experience I laugh and I cringe. I was innocent and stupid and gullible and needy and real. Just what a teenager is supposed to be. I would have loved for my first time to be romantic and perfect and sweet. I had visions of rose petals and soft music and a cool summer breeze floating through the half opened bedroom window through which my lover had just secretly climbed. We would make sweet love on Egyptian cotton sheets until the perfect sunrise lit the room. Some women may get that. I don't think most do.

The first piece of advice I would give to any woman considering losing her virginity in this day and age would be to protect herself. Get a prescription for birth control pills and follow that with a healthy dose of condoms. Your heart may think he is the right man for you but your heart will heal faster than an unwanted pregnancy or AIDS. Secondly and this may seem cliché, the right man will wait for you. You are under no obligation to share your body with anyone for any reason. Love and respect yourself first before you look for love and respect. You will always remember your first time. You want that memory to be a good one. When you find the right person to share yourself with it will be a truly wonderful, one of a kind experience. And lastly, keep in mind that guys have first experiences as well. And chances are they are or have been unsure and nervous about sex as well. Actually, trust me, they ARE unsure and nervous, probably more than women. But they will never admit it. And that may be to our advantage.

As for good ole' Jonah, I didn't see or speak to him for nearly a year. When our paths crossed again I was in between boyfriends, so I invited him up to my "I am so cool" college apartment. He had been seeing a woman who was at least ten years older than him and lived down the street from his house. I didn't ask about her. We smoked a joint on my balcony and laughed about pink elephants flying by (but really were not). I wanted to have sex with him again. I am not sure why. Maybe to show him how much I had improved. I doubt if he would have noticed. He left before we had a chance.

A few years later I moved out of state and a few years after that, I moved back. Last year I saw him in the *Wedding* section of the local paper. He had married (first? second? third?). He looked the same except he had no hair (shaved or lost I could not tell). She was a plain looking girl whose name sounded familiar. A few weeks later I saw an article in the *Lifestyles* section of the local paper written by her. That was the connection. Now, every few weeks or so I can read about him. She loves to talk about their travels/home/meals like every newlywed does and they sound so happy. It is surreal. I know where he has been, where he lives and what he eats. I wonder if he remembers that night or me. And I wonder if he has a daughter of his own.

My view of sex afterwards was that I wanted to wait 'til I found the right girl and not a one-night stand.

Male: I am 26. I was 19, a late bloomer.

It was totally unexpected. I had been at a bar one night with a friend and it was just a girl who I knew from other friends. We ended up walking home and one thing led to another. It wasn't how I expected to have sex for the first time—outdoors.

She was friends with my group of friends but went to another high school. She was one year older than I am and more experienced. I'd known her for a few years but we didn't hang out.

I had no advice from my parents. That's a topic that was never brought up. I can't remember what I heard from friends. I knew people were doing it but never got into details. There was no advice from religious figures either. I was too scared to ask.

We did it outside in the grass in front of some person's house. It was around three in the morning and right by the road, so we ducked if we heard a car coming.

It was a total surprise. I thought we were just walking home and then she asked if I wanted to have sex. I'd never done it, I was drunk and I said yes. We didn't use birth control because it was a surprise. She might have been on it but I didn't wear a condom.

It actually happened pretty fast. Well, it being the first time, you know it didn't last that long. I had a hard time getting it in and I think I was thinking "Don't cum, please don't cum." She helped me guide it in and then, to my surprise, I came.

I was totally respectful of her and what was going on. I walked her home afterward. She asked if I was a virgin and I said, "Nope. Just nervous."

The best part was it felt good, warm and wet and I couldn't believe I was doing it, so I was happy. The worst part was that it didn't last longer. I regretted that but, oh well, it was too late to dwell on something I couldn't change.

I didn't really tell anyone because I didn't know her that well and I was drunk. But then I heard people knew, so I told some friends and we joked about it.

After that night we never hung out. I saw her a few times at parties and we had a good laugh about it. I moved from that town, so I probably won't run into her anytime soon.

My view of sex afterwards was that I wanted to wait 'til I found the right girl and not a one-night stand. I was young and having fun and now I look back on it and laugh.

My advice to virgins is to do it with someone you care about.

I'm just lucky I didn't get pregnant, being dumb enough to listen to him, a teenaged guy, instruct me about birth control!

Female: I am currently 35 years old. I was 16 when I lost my virginity.

I guess I didn't have any real expectation of how I wanted it to be but I certainly didn't have any unrealistic romantic version of it in my head. I think that when I'd thought about what it would be like, I pictured it to be a bit dangerous, edgy and somewhat forbidden.

He was a friend of my cousin and I had known him since I was about ten or eleven. He was two and a half years older than me and I had always had a crush on him and suspected he liked me as well. I moved around a lot in my early teens and he always wrote letters to me wherever I was. He was very creative and a bit of a rebel in his own way and "bad boys" had always appealed to me. I moved back into his area when I was sixteen. I saw him at a school play and we sat together. He put his hand on my leg and the sparks flew. I knew then that he would eventually be the one.

We dated for a month or so before we took that next step. I remember it was winter and one day we didn't have school, either because it was a snow day or because of teacher's conferences. I was over at his house and his parents were at work, so we had the place to ourselves. I knew that would be the day. He was experienced and was very caring with me. He made sure I was comfortable and he went very slowly. Unfortunately, just as we were about to do it, his mother came home and we stopped before going any further. We tried again, more successfully, a few days later.

Historical records show that even in 1850 B.C., women attempted to practice birth control. The most common method was a mixture of crocodile dung and honey placed in the vagina in the hopes of preventing pregnancy.
- Baker, JoAnn and Erica Orloff. 2001. Dirty Little Secrets: True Tales and Twisted Trivia about Sex. New York, NY: MacMillan Publishing Company, Inc.
Source: www.randomhistory.com

He was quite big and it hurt a lot but there was no trouble getting it in. I think I may have cried, mainly from the shock of such a new and intimate act. But I was happy to have finally done it and with him of all people. We cuddled afterwards and lounged around his house and drank hot tea for the rest of the day and it was wonderful. We didn't use any kind of birth control, other than withdrawal. Actually, for most of our relationship we didn't use anything. He felt he was an expert in everything and told me that I couldn't get pregnant in the week before or the week after my period. I'm just lucky I didn't get pregnant, being dumb enough to listen to him, a teenaged guy, instruct me about birth control!

The best part of losing my virginity was having that intimate connection to someone I cared so much about. The worst part was having to sneak around from my parents.

I never regretted any of it. I didn't tell anyone about it afterwards because there really wasn't anyone to tell. My friends were very naïve and I thought that they would think I was a slut, mainly because they couldn't get a boyfriend themselves.

We dated on and off for the next two or three years and in that time I discovered that, while I was so drawn to him and so in love with him, he was very arrogant and felt that our relationship was never mutually exclusive. He deflowered another girl and began dating her as well as me. He made it seem that I shouldn't have any sort of problem with that and I was naïve enough to believe him, even though I was torn up about it.

Eventually I was strong enough to make that break and not date him anymore. He was really sad and cried but I think mainly it was because it was a blow to his ego to have someone reject him. I saw him around several times over the years and we stayed on friendly terms. I still think about him a lot and I know he thinks about me as well. We have known each other for too long and were very close for too long to ever forget.

My idea of sex became a way to have a physical, intimate relationship with someone. I guess this may have had to do with my young age at which I lost my virginity. It also may have had to do with the fact that he controlled my emotions completely during the time we dated. I didn't feel that sex had to be combined with love. Sex was just sex. It was an ego boost for me to know I was desired enough by a guy for us to have that intimate contact, even if it was just once. I became somewhat promiscuous in the years following our relationship.

I don't recall ever getting any advice from my parents regarding sex. Which seems kind of odd. My parents were quite young and maybe they didn't know quite how to approach it with me. Of course, they were nineteen when they had me, so they probably should have had something to say on the subject!

Most of my friends were also virgins. I was afraid to talk to them about sex because they didn't seem too likely to experience it in the near future. They had no realistic chances with any of the boys we knew and I would have been very, very surprised if any of them had gotten a boyfriend. I was the first one (and only one in the time that we were in high school together!) to have a boyfriend, or to have sex.

There were no religious figures in my life, so I didn't get any kind of religious advice at all. I had attended a school run by fundamentalist Christian missionaries at one point in my travels and their outlook on most things was that if you didn't do what they said you'd go to hell, so I pretty much took everything they preached with a grain of salt.

Now that I am older, I look back on the experience in a positive light. I was miserable in all my teen angst stuff but all in all, it was a good experience. It was with someone I knew and trusted and liked (and who was probably destined to have been my first) and it was in an environment where I was comfortable (his house). I don't think I would have changed anything. I'm also glad that I was so young when I did it. I got married when I was twenty-three (and have still been happily married ever since!) and I felt that I had already experienced all the situations and relationships and sexual encounters that I needed to feel ready to take the big step. I didn't feel like I was missing out on anything.

I don't necessarily advise for virgins to do what I did. I think waiting may be a better idea for a lot of people. I felt ready at that age to do it and I think it was beneficial for me but I would definitely advise that they do what they feel is right. They need to feel that they are strong enough to handle the flood of emotions that goes along with the loss of virginity and they need to be sure that the person that they are planning on doing it with is someone they know and trust.

I *haven't spoken to her in almost ten years but to this day, I can still remember what she wore that night.*

Male: I am 26. I was 16 when I lost my virginity.

I didn't know what to expect, honestly. I knew by watching movies and magazines what to do, just the basic stuff, nothing fancy. She was one of my ex-girlfriend's friends. She was a little older than me, not by much though. I believe she was seventeen. I had known her for about one and a half years.

My parents just told me to be careful and to use protection. Which I didn't do. I didn't get any advice from friends, just heard from those who had already had sex what they had done. Not too much into religion, so no advice.

It was at the house of a friend who I had a crush on. We were all in her room and she was on the bed with her boyfriend making out and me and the other girl were lying on the floor making out. Once things got hot, we went to the spare bedroom. I didn't know it was going to happen. I was taken by surprise. She told me to go to the other bedroom and she would follow. When she got in there, she took off my shirt and my shorts and then she led me to the bed. I was like, Oh my god, is this really happening!

I believe and I say again, believe she was on birth control. I didn't use a condom.

I was pretty amazed. It felt pretty good. But I don't think that I could ever have known what it would have felt like just thinking about it. I never got sad or scared. Just plain out amazed!

I would have to say that I was sweet and gentle and at the same time it was a little awkward for me.

She didn't know I was a virgin at the time. I didn't tell her until we started dating. But she said she didn't even know, so I must think that I was pretty good. There was no trouble at all getting it in. The best part for me was being inside her and having my naked body against hers. The worst part was finishing.

I felt pretty good. Like I had just stepped into the real man world. I had liked her before this encounter. I wouldn't say that I loved her, just liked her a lot.

Hell yeah I told people. I grabbed my friend and we went outside for a smoke and I told him what happened. Nothing in detail though! He knew that I was a virgin.

She and I broke up a few months later. She got married and moved on with her life. I haven't spoken to her in almost ten years but to this day, I can still remember what she wore that night.

Honestly I didn't choose it. It was just something that happened. No regrets of course.

It made me want to have sex more and more. Over the years I can say that my sex drive has declined a little but not much.

I look back and just smile. It was something that I enjoyed very much. I wouldn't change a thing!

My advice is to just make sure you are comfortable with the person you lose it with. I don't believe that you have to love that person.

I got the scare of my life afterward. Someone told me that she was pregnant because she was late on her period but it turned out to be nothing.

I just sort of laid there and waited for him to finish and wondered what was going on that he was having so much fun.

Female: I am 58 years old. I was 18 when I finally went all the way.

Up until then I had indulged in the usual teenage practices of making out and heavy petting but my Catholic upbringing, coupled with the fear of pregnancy, had effectively put the brakes on anything more. Not that I wasn't curious. I most certainly was (who wasn't?), not to mention being more than just a little jealous of those who already possessed the forbidden knowledge. I had no particular expectations. It was something I figured I had to get out of the way. I was also a little scared because I had no access to birth control, which was a brand new technology. I just wanted to see what all the fuss was about.

The extent of my sex education was my mother giving me a booklet titled *Now You Are Ten* with regard to having my period. I suppose I was lucky because I've met other women who thought they had cancer when they first got their period and were extremely traumatized until it was explained to them that it was a normal thing. I recall asking my mother once where babies came from and she became visibly uncomfortable. To her credit, she decided I needed an answer, so she told me that when two people loved each other, they got married and were very close. This closeness was what produced a baby. End of story.

I knew I wasn't supposed to have sex because when you attend Catholic school for twelve years it is pounded into your head on a daily basis that sex is for procreation only and even when you're married, having sex for fun is somehow scandalous. Also, my unmarried older sister had become pregnant back in the late 50s and there was no mistaking my parents' reaction to that. She was literally told to leave the house. My father wouldn't even sleep in the house while she was there—he went out and slept in the car. So I guess the advice given to me in an oblique way was NO WAY!

Nobody talked about sex in anything other than whispers and then it was always more of a wondering what it was all about rather than anything from experience or factual. When I was a freshman in high school, one of the girls got pregnant and didn't come back the next year. Everyone spoke about her in hushed tones and I think that underneath our shock, there was also a curiosity and a strange sort of envy that she had knowledge we didn't possess. But at least we weren't "knocked up". The nuns never mentioned her.

The advice I got from religious figures (nuns mainly) was that sex is sinful. Even between a husband and wife it was something not to be discussed. It was the duty of the wife, giving it a somewhat unfavorable impression. Mostly, sex is sinful and sort of icky. Period.

My first sexual partner was a boy I'd met while out with my girlfriend. I had a back problem and was on prescription pain medication and my friend and I were walking home when these two boys pulled up next to us and started flirting. I was really gone on the medication and I kept advising my girlfriend to ignore them. But each time the boy sitting shotgun spoke, I would answer. My girlfriend kept saying, "come on, let's go home" and I would turn and advise her to ignore those boys, telling her that now they would want us to come over to the car. They did and I dragged her over, all the time telling her that they would then want us to get into the car and under no circumstances should we do that. The cute one sitting shotgun asked us if we wanted to go for a ride and I, of course, not heeding my own advice, said "sure!" and dragged my friend along. Once in the car, we found out they'd been thrown out of their senior class party for drinking. This made them daring in my eyes. And I really thought the one was cute. We wound up in a cemetery, where they stopped to go pee. I had a bad moment then, thinking perhaps being in a graveyard at night with two strange boys might not be such a great idea and I kept on giving advice to my girlfriend, who by this time had decided I was out of my mind. However, she remained my friend and we laughed about it years later. The boys took us home, no harm, no foul and the cute one called me. But it took him two weeks to do so and I thought he'd forgotten about me. I think the reason was that he got punished for getting thrown out of the school party for being drunk.

I'd known him for about two years when we consummated our relationship. We had "gone steady" for awhile the year before but he dumped me because I wouldn't "put out". He was nineteen. We'd started going out again just recently. Interestingly enough, at the time we started dating again I was going to school with the girl he'd dumped me for. She still liked him and I think I used the fact that we were dating again to lord it over her.

We did it on a dirty old bed in a dirty old farmhouse out in the country past the state line at a party with a lot of drunken kids. I was the only sober one there. I kind of suspected it would happen. I wasn't certain when but the opportunity presented itself and we did it. It really wasn't all that exciting. I remember opening my eyes and looking around at the surroundings and thinking they weren't exactly my idea of the perfect place to lose my virginity. I was afraid somebody would come in while we were doing it. Everybody was outside sitting around a big bonfire and drinking.

It didn't hurt because years earlier, when I was about five or six, I'd been walking on an iron railing that separated my front porch from the one next door and I slipped and fell spread eagle on the railing. To this day I wince when I think of it. It really hurt. I remember that there was blood in my underwear when that happened. Years later, when I had sex for the first time, I didn't bleed and then realized that I'd broken my hymen back when I fell. Sex didn't hurt but it didn't feel particularly good either. I just sort of laid there and waited for him to finish and wondered what was going on that he was having so much fun. For me it was just sort of blah and something to get out of the way. As for him, I don't think he had any respect or disrespect for me. He was nineteen and in a hurry and that about sums it up. The best word to describe his performance would have to be urgent. He was urgent! I honestly don't remember if he had trouble getting it in. There really was not a best and worst part, except I was glad when it was over and a bit disappointed, I suppose, because it was such a non-event.

Like I said, I had no birth control. Nope. No way I could get it in the mid-60s without my parents knowing about it. Ha! Like that would happen! Just to give you an inkling of what I was up against, my mother didn't want me to use tampons because she thought that they would harm me somehow. I hadn't even been to a gynecologist. I finally got birth control when I became engaged (to the boy with whom I'd lost my virginity). My fiancé wasn't even around then, as he was in the military and stationed on the other side of the country and I got birth control a couple of months before we got married because I'd heard that you had to be taking it for awhile before it became effective.

Afterward, I felt scared because I was convinced that I'd gotten pregnant. I mean, almost immediately afterwards, I started checking to see if I got my period. The next day I felt like everyone could tell by looking at me that I'd "done it". Felt like I had a big red neon "A" (for adultery, like in that story *The Scarlet Letter*) plastered across my forehead.

The experience didn't alter my feelings about him one way or the other.

I didn't feel like I was madly in love with him, nor did I resent him for taking advantage of me. He hadn't. It was definitely a two-way street. It wasn't really about him, it was more about me wanting to experience what was such a mystery and so forbidden. I chose to lose my virginity at that time because I just figured it was time. You know, eat, drink and be merry for tomorrow you die.

I told my best friend who lived next door to me. She'd already had sex with her boyfriend. It wasn't the same back then as it is now. We didn't talk about the particulars, just about the fact that we'd done it. It made us feel more like women as opposed to girls. I guess we viewed it as a rite of passage.

I married and divorced him. And we still exchange Christmas cards. When I'm in town, he's apt to invite me over for dinner with his wife and family. We've remained friends of a sort, although we would really never seek each other out. But we had a child together and it's kept us in touch over the years.

That experience itself didn't color my attitude toward sex. I think my attitude towards sex, which I still haven't really figured out, has been shaped by the cumulative experiences I've had through the years. One thing has made itself very clear: most men don't have a clue how to satisfy a woman—there are notable exceptions—and aren't really interested in finding out how to. This, you must understand, is just my observation based on the number of men I've bedded. Although some wouldn't count it as a matter of pride, my experience has been somewhat extensive. I "grew up" in the pre-AIDS sex and drugs and rock 'n roll era of the 60' and 70s. I graduated high school in 1965, which was a time on the cusp of a great shift in the mores surrounding sex. My marriage ended in the early 70s and at that time everyone—at least everyone I knew—was having sex with everyone else. As for experiences that shaped my attitude, I found that some men surprised me with their sexual prowess while others literally put me to sleep right in the middle of the act. I also found that an inordinate number of men were able to forget their wives and children when the urge overtook them. So I would suppose you could say I'm somewhat jaded. Add to that twelve years of Catholic school and the crap they shoveled out regarding sex and it's a wonder I'm not a babbling idiot.

Looking back I say: You gotta start somewhere! I think incredibly romantic, exciting, earth-shattering first time sex is a myth that only happens in badly written romance novels. Having sex for the first time is something that even today scares girls to some extent and maybe boys too but in a different way. I think it's really important that you have your first sexual experience when you feel you're ready, not when someone pressures you into it

As first times go, mine was probably about average. I think the true revelation about sex for me predated my first actual penetration. It was several months earlier and I let a boy go down on me—something I had never heard of—but I found that I sure did like it. Poor guy. He worked so hard and then I wouldn't let him get his. And in the end, I think that's the thing that puts a smile on my face. In all my battles with men, that's probably one of the few times I felt I had the upper hand!

*T*o me her reaction looked like disappointment.

Male: I am 25. I was 14.

I really didn't have any expectations. I was very curious to know what it felt like. She was my first love—my first girlfriend (lasted about a year). I knew her for approximately three years.

My parents told me to always use protection—nothing beyond that. My friends didn't give me any advice. Just a lot of people boasting that they had done it but no details. They were most were likely lying. I didn't get any advice from a religious figure.

I was home on vacation from an all male boarding school. It was my last chance to lose my virginity before turning fifteen. We'd had plenty of phone sex and that was what kept us intimate with one another. I stole my mother's car in the middle of the night and drove about twenty miles to her house. She snuck me into her bedroom. We might have used a condom. I really don't remember.

> *Remember, if you smoke after sex you're doing it too fast.*
> *- Woody Allen*
> *Source: www.quotesdaddy.com*

I was very excited. But my mind was preoccupied with technique, thinking, "How should I be doing this? Do I go fast or slow? Does she like it?" I kept questioning her as to what she liked. What, if anything, did she want done differently? I had some trouble getting it in until I figured out she needed to be wet. But she was experienced with masturbating. Using objects like cucumbers and the like. So fit was not an issue.

To me her reaction looked like disappointment. It was her first time as well.

The best part was the foreplay. I still remember that the most vividly. The worst part was realizing that my penis was not big enough for her. A fourteen-year-old's penis usually doesn't measure up to a fat cucumber.

It felt a little awkward. Kind of like "that's it?" I was expecting a more ethereal experience. I was madly in love with her.

I don't recall telling anyone about it but I'm sure I told my friends.

The last I heard, she is in a lesbian relationship with an older woman. I haven't spoken with her in about four or five years.

I chose to lose my virginity with her at that time because I was a very horny kid. I just wanted to lose it. It was not at all something emotional. As for coloring my attitude towards sex, no, it didn't.

I have no regrets at all. Looking back I think it's a little funny. I wouldn't change anything about it. I think the way it turned out was the way it was meant to be and I'm totally fine with it.

Any advice I would have to offer would revolve around technique, so you wouldn't have to be too nervous and be able to enjoy the experience. I have nothing to offer in regards to an emotional level of maturity, holding out or anything like that.

I would say it felt horrible yet great, painful yet awesome, scary yet empowering.

Female: I'm 61 years old. I was 25.

Here it is. My first encounter. I grew up in an austere Catholic environment, attending an all-girls Catholic school, where we were taught to believe even a passionate kiss was a sin. I was determined to remain a virgin until my wedding day. It wasn't easy. Guys would always make me feel that I had to give them what they wanted to stay in a relationship. When a guy left because I said no, I really wanted to drop my values. But I painfully hung tight.

When I was twenty-five and still a virgin, my mother put me through so much trauma with her alcoholism. I decided to move to New York and try the Big Apple. It was a scary change but I was determined to make it. I met a friend through my work and we became roommates. She talked me into going with her and some friends to a dude ranch in upstate New York. It was truly one of the most memorable and fun weekends of my life. I met Duke, the singer in the band, among other job titles there. We married only three months later. It was a whirlwind romance. Every weekend I would travel from the city to spend the weekend with him. He called me every night. He was a perfect gentleman though. He proposed to me in August. We were two weeks away from our wedding date.

Duke started pushing for more than just necking. He promised he was so sincere about marrying me. Why did we have to wait? After a very romantic evening on the dance floor, he escorted me to my room at the ranch. His kisses broke down my resistance. I was scared but so excited. And I was so anxious for him to be happy and pleased with me. I felt self-conscious but his arms around me and his soft whispers in my ear made me feel warm and safe and loved. So I would say it felt horrible yet great, painful yet awesome, scary yet empowering.

I felt a lot of guilt and fear afterwards. What if he did not go ahead with our marriage? What if I got pregnant? My family and friends would know the bad thing I did!

Duke sensed my pain. He confirmed his love for me. Our wedding day was the most special day of my life. And it made an "honest woman" of me. Ha Ha.

***H**er friends told me she was a huge slut. This turned me on because I knew it would take very little work to nail her.*

Male: I'm 23. I was 19.

I had no expectations. I only knew that my body had been pushing me to do it since about age fourteen. There was no peer pressure involved. I just wanted to get laid so badly and when the opportunity presented itself, I was on it like stink on shit.

She was a high school senior who was visiting my college campus for a concert. We had one common friend who invited a group of her friends to stay in our dorm room. I met her that very night, before the show. She was a high school girl. Me a college boy. I think she was a little turned on by the "older guy" thing. We got drunk and hooked up after the concert. We knew each other for eight hours before we had sex.

My parents didn't give me any advice. They never discussed "the birds and the bees." My dad once offered to explain things when I was about eleven or twelve. I declined and that was that. One of my friends told me that after he lost his virginity his brain kept saying, "Let's do it again." That rung in my head for years and years until I finally got laid. Interestingly enough, I didn't want to "do it again." I just wanted to make sure that the condom didn't break. I was and still am, terrified about pregnancy. I mean, I want kids but only in the context of love and marriage.

As for religious advice, I really didn't get any. Well, maybe. I'm sure a few Catholic priests explained why one should remain celibate until marriage. I tend to agree with them. But we live in a society of immediate gratification and, as I said earlier, I did not act based on peer pressure. My body was about to explode and I couldn't resist.

We did it on the floor. It was so hot. I wasn't expecting it at all. The situation just happened. We made out, our clothes came off slowly and just enough to do it. We used a condom. She also claimed to be on the pill but I didn't know her well enough to verify this claim.

I wasn't scared but I was definitely happy and when I came I was in a state of complete euphoria. I was gentle, awkward, sweet and I was also quick. I probably lasted about seventy-five seconds. She was enjoying it but probably wanted more.

I didn't have much trouble getting it in. She helped a lot. I knew that she was experienced because her friends told me she was a huge slut. This turned me on because I knew it would take very little work to nail her. When you're a nineteen-year-old virgin, this is a big turn-on. We don't think of it as taking advantage, we think of it as doing what we gotta do.

The best part was coming. The worst part was wondering what would have happened if the condom broke. I barely knew her. Our homes were hundreds of mile away and I don't believe in abortion.

Afterwards I felt some regret but mostly relief. She was sweet but I had no interest in her as a long-term girlfriend.

Most of my friends knew because they were in the room hooking up with other girls. It was nearly an orgy except that we were coupled off.

I don't know what happened to her. Her friend called one of my friends one time but I avoided the situation. I didn't want to date her.

I chose to lose my virginity with her because my body was surging with hormones/desire/testosterone. I can't really offer any other explanation. I wouldn't have sex for those reasons at my current age but as a nineteen-year-old virgin, those things dictated my actions.

That experience made me more comfortable with sex. I didn't feel so awkward about it. The next time a girl was really coming on to me, I had the confidence to "hook up" or "close the deal", whereas before that first sexual experience I was awkward, scared and even worried.

I wish I had remained a virgin and slept with a real girlfriend but there are other times when I'm happy that I practiced for the real thing. All of my girlfriends have loved me in bed and had I waited, I might have been bad in bed, or too quick/awkward/nerdy. I needed to lose my virginity to get into a comfort zone.

I probably wouldn't change anything about my first experience. If I had met my dream girl and got married, I would have wished that I never slept with anyone else. But that hasn't been the case. I've had three serious girlfriends, so the whole whimsical ideal of being with one person is gone.

My advice to virgins is to utilize masturbation. It will always be there for you. Don't be ashamed to pleasure yourself. It's healthy and safe, plus you can be with anyone you want when you use your imagination.

From my friends I heard that if you did it standing up, you wouldn't get pregnant.

Female: I'll be 23 next month. I was 17 then.

My expectations of losing my virginity were that it was to be something special, with somebody that was special. Same as every girl.

He was some guy, I don't really know. He was a guy that hung out with a party group I was in. I have no idea how old he was. He doesn't even remember doing it because he was on acid.

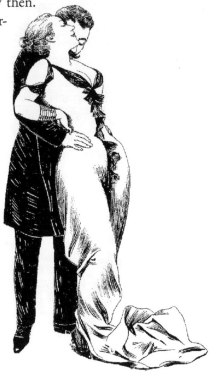

I knew of him. I never really talked to him before. It was just one of those things that I don't know how it happened, it just happened. I was with my best friend at the time. It started as a bet. Everyone thought he was gay cause he was kind of fruity looking. And he danced really good. We had never seen him with a girl. I didn't think he was (gay). I thought he was really cute. We were drinking and the more I drank I was like, "How much do you want to bet he isn't gay?"

We were on my uncle's porch when we did it. People were around but they didn't see because they were all busy making out. We were under a blanket trying to stay warm. That's how it led us to doing it.

It didn't go very far because like I said, he was on acid and it was soft. It was horrible. I remember thinking it was messy, it felt yucky. He grossed me out because I started to sober up and I realized what I was doing. It was so gross. I didn't like it at all. He wasn't respectful and he was awkward. He was on acid so it was like he was there but he wasn't there, (like he was) in another world. It took a long time to get it in.

The best part was after a while I kind of wised up. I was happy that I didn't like it because I would have gotten into a lot more trouble. We didn't use birth control because I hadn't planned on doing it. The worst part was that it was horrible. I didn't even know his name. It turned into this big thing: My uncle tried to kill him. My uncle showed up and had found out and he ran upstairs to where the guy I did it with was. He was passed out on the top of the stairs. My uncle grabbed him and hung him out of the second story window. One of my other friends tried to calm my uncle down. Afterward, I told everybody, do not do the grown-up. Save it for the right person. WAIT!

My parents wanted me to wait until I was married. It was a really religious household.

From my friends I heard that if you did it standing up, you wouldn't get pregnant. That if you washed off right after, you wouldn't get pregnant.

My church de-fellowshipped me for a year. I was punished and wasn't allowed to talk to any of my friends for a while. I guess my friends leaked some of the information about it and some parents overheard. When I was confronted, I didn't deny it.

My friends who weren't virgins had it built up so much, I was so disappointed. They talked about the orgasm and all this stuff. I didn't have an orgasm. It hurt. After, I was sore, then I was just like "This sucks!"

I didn't do it for a long time, years later. I waited until I was nineteen and then I got pregnant.

I saw him about a month ago at the mall. I don't think he recognized me and I didn't say anything. I was with my boyfriend. It was so weird. It meant nothing. I didn't care to even say hi.

The experience made me wait and now I am more vocal, like I'll say "No, I don't like that." I speak up more.

My advice is to wait, take your time. It's something that will come in it's own time. Don't rush it. I know girls who are sixteen now and they're too ahead of their time.

My mom was right when she told me it's something special and it really is. And I think once you learn to respect yourself then you'll be ready and I don't think a sixteen or seventeen year old girl really knows how to respect herself. They're still learning.

This next story was answered before we sent the questionnaire. We emailed him to thank him and to let him know there was an official list of questions and that in comparison his story would fall short of the other ones we had received. He emailed back and wrote, "I didn't realize this was a contest." We explained as nicely as we could that it isn't a contest, just that there were more questions. We never heard from him again. After a bit of consideration, we've decided to include it.

I *didn't know what the hell I was doing and luckily, because I was drunk and did not care about her, I wasn't embarrassed.*

Male: I'm 43. I lost my virginity when I was 18 years old to a girl I didn't even like.

She went to a different high school and was a freshman. I was drinking and partying a lot at the time, so the details aren't as clear as they could be. All I know is that two of my friends and I had been sneaking this girl out of her house for a few months and messing around with her. I didn't have any feelings towards her and just thought of her as a plaything to mess with when we were bored, drunk and horny late at night.

I remember sneaking her out one night and right when she was getting in our car, her brother came running out of her house carrying a baseball bat, screaming at us. We took off and went to my friend's house at about 2:00 am in the morning. His parents were gone on a trip and he had the run of the place. I remember getting drunk and taking this girl into my friend's bedroom, as I had many times before. I didn't know what the hell I was doing and luckily, because I was drunk and did not care about her, I wasn't embarrassed. I remember my friends laughing, yelling and knocking on the door while I was losing my virginity.

It was surreal and hardly romantic in any way. I completed what I was doing and walked out of the room and partied with my friends some more while she stayed in the bedroom.

I found out later that night that she was a virgin too and really liked me a lot. I didn't care one way or the other, not because that's my personality, I just had a world of other more important things on my mind, like what the hell I was going to do with the rest of my life.

I remember we were kissing and I felt like Beaver learning about kissing through Wally.

Female: I'm 20. I was 18.

I had no expectations other than to be convinced I'd be a virgin forever. He was a friend of a friend and was twenty-two.

My sister outed me in the eighth grade. I fought the idea that I was gay and not until I was nineteen did I accept it. So having sex with that guy didn't do anything for me except make me sore. I knew him for probably a little over five hours.

My parents gave me no advice at all. I'm very surprised my mother didn't. All she did was tell stories about her past. NO advice though. I don't remember advice or rumors from my friends. But I'd been through Sex Ed so many times, most of the dumb stuff floating around completely missed me. I didn't get any advice from religious figures either.

We did it in the front seat of his car. Horrible, horrible experience. I was stoned on MaryJane and he kept talking. His talking pissed me off, so I just said. " You got a condom?" He did and it went down after that. So I can't say it was a surprise.

I remember we were kissing and I felt like Beaver learning about kissing through Wally. It was a very strange, tripped-out, almost out of body experience. Except for the fact that it hurt—a lot. He had a lot of trouble getting it in, so much so that I made him stop probably twenty minutes into it. I remember giggling like crazy because afterwards he bought me two honey buns and a soft drink.

I was very awkward. I didn't move that much. I didn't say anything. Afterwards, he wanted to be my boyfriend, which really surprised me. I wanted it to be a one-night stand.

The best part was not being a virgin anymore and the fact that I did it stoned. I learned a lot about myself that week. The worst was that he stuck around for another two months.

My feeling afterwards was pride because I participated in the act that created the world. As for him, I couldn't care less. Not at the time, not now.

I told everyone but my mama.

My mother ended up letting him live with us for three months. I don't know where he is now.

I chose to lose my virginity with him at that time because I had the opportunity.

I guess the experience did color my attitude toward sex. Sex never really meant anything to me. Then after having sex I found out, it really meant nothing to me. Even though it felt really good.

Now that I'm older, I look back on that experience and I think, who was that person who had sex with that loser?

If I had it to do all over again, I wouldn't have slept with him, I would have waited for my first girl friend.

My advice to virgins is this: After you have sex for the first time, never sleep with a virgin guy. It's the most awkward, traumatic thing ever.

My friends called me Terminator, except that I was very sweet and polite.

Male: I'm 35 years old and when I lost my virginity I was 16.

I was a great teenager: always trying to help, very active and happy. I played football in high school. I weighed one hundred eighty-five pounds and my height was 5'10". I was very strong. My friends called me Terminator, except that I was very sweet and polite.

Everything happened unexpectedly one day around noon. The woman who took my virginity away was my uncle's wife. She was beautiful, with a great rounded ass. She was thirty-something and had moved next door a couple years before. Sometimes when I went up to the roof I could see her in her backyard doing the laundry. Other times she came into my house and talked to my mother for hours, of course always when I was there.

My parents always gave us our freedom, no restrictions but some rules, like always come home, don't do drugs and don't steal. My parents never talked about sexual stuff and we were not allowed to discuss it or to be obscene in the house. A little conservative I must say.

I grew up on the street, so I knew everything about sexuality at that age. Even some of my friends had already taken me to see and to be with the prostitutes (another amazing story) but I was disgusted. They did it but not me. I was smarter than that. I'm Catholic and in the church they taught me about sacraments, sins and fornication. Of course I knew when it was okay and not okay to have sex with somebody.

One day I was on the roof of my house playing with my dog and I saw my neighbor doing her laundry like I always did. This time she called me, shouting my name.

"Yes, what do you want?"

"Can you come here and fix my iron's plug?"

"Of course."

So I climbed down the ladder, went to her house and she took me into her bedroom, pulled out the iron from the closet and showed me what needed to be done. It was very simple. I needed a screwdriver, electrical tape and pliers. She got them for me and told me to sit on her bed. So I started to fix the iron and she stood up in front of me, watching me. I was a little nervous because I don't like people watching over me. She kept watching me and then she asked me, "Do you find me attractive?"

I was shy but I said, "Of course." (She was not very pretty but had a great body, maybe all that washing by hand.)

She took the pliers and the iron from my hands and got close to me and started to touch my hair. Later she held my hands and put them on her sweet round butt (maybe that's the reason why I like to squeeze women's butts when I have sex with them). She pulled back and took her panties off. Everything was so surprising

I was very awkward. She held my hips and pushed them out a little and then pulled them back and she told me to do it like that—out and in. Then I came for the first time without masturbating. This feeling was unreal, so sublime. I felt like I was in heaven. She kept kissing me for awhile. Tears came from her eyes and I was worried. She smiled at me, got up, put her blouse on and walked out of the room to the bathroom. She had stuck her nails in my back, leaving marks that I didn't notice but I did later when I took a shower. I was worried about getting her pregnant because I knew that that is how it happens.

In the middle 80s in Mexico we did not use condoms. The women did all the birth control on their own. I was a little worried but so happy. I had sex with my uncle's wife! I finished fixing the iron's plug and she gave me money. I said no but she put it in my jeans pocket. After all, I needed it to have fun at school. She gave me a very sensual kiss and I left. That was the worst part. I wanted to stay and be with her again. But I was so happy and proud. You see I didn't need prostitutes to find out what is like to love a woman. Ever since then I worship them. I think about the intense pleasure that any of them can offer.

Our relationship continued for many months and through my sister I found out that my uncle only had sex with my aunt when he was drunk. (Since then I have disliked my uncle. I wanted to break his face.) Luckily, I found the most amazing woman in my high school and started to go out with her and, little by little, I forgot about my uncle's wife.

A few years later they moved to another neighborhood and one day she came to visit my family. Nobody was there except me and we did it on my room's carpet. That was it. I never saw her again until two years ago in one of my trips to Mexico. She came to see me with my uncle. It was nice; he was not drinking anymore. I did not ask anything about their sexual life.

I'm very happy that she was the one. I will always remember her and I will thank her eternally for those precious and unforgettable moments.

Besides football and sports, sex became my obsession. Freud was right! I lived for it until I found my other loves: philosophy and my wife.

I would never change anything, not a single moment. Everything that happened was beautiful and I also thank life. I want to tell my story to any virgins out there because sex is beautiful when you do it with the right intentions and if you are lucky to find a great lover. If not, keep searching. For example, I had had better sex with many women than with my wife. But my wife is an amazing person and I love her so dearly that I can't describe my love for her. Love is not about sex, sex is about love. You see Freud was a little short of understanding why sex is sublime and transcendental.

I ***realized that I had better learn to speak up or suffer the consequences.***

Female: I am currently 31 years old. I was 15 when I lost my virginity.

It was a few months before my sixteenth birthday and at the time I kept reminding myself of that fact. For some reason, being fifteen seemed far too young for me to be having sex but sixteen seemed appropriate. So, I justified the experience by saying I'll be sixteen in two months so it's okay.

I don't really know what I was expecting to happen. My parents had cable and I had seen sex on TV and had an idea of what it should look like. I had also read some books about sex but they were all very clinical and boring. So I knew what would happen physically but I still don't think I knew what exactly would happen. I remember wanting it to mean something. I also remember that I wanted to get it over with in a way, because everyone talks about it and puts so much weight on whether or not you are a virgin. But at the same time, I really wanted it to be with the boy I was with. I loved him very much and

I thought that because I loved him so much, that it was okay that we have sex.

I had been in love with him for about a year. He was gorgeous to me! Tall, beautiful blue eyes, funny and we had so much in common. We were dating in my mind but now that I look back on it all, I have my doubts. I think I was more in love with him than he was with me. I know that he loved me too but he was very selfish at the time. We were in school together and were really good friends. He was the same age as me and he was a virgin too. We had known each other for almost two years before we slept together.

My parents really didn't give me much advice about sex. I distinctly remember being around thirteen or fourteen years old and having these books appear on our bookshelf. They were about reproduction and sex and had pictures and diagrams of penises and vaginas and were very informative. I also remember that they were specifically for young adults because the glossary had slang terms listed so you could look up dick if you didn't know the correct word. I remember that these books magically appeared one day and were placed on the shelf that was neither too high up nor too low down. It was like they were placed on the shelf that was at just the right level that a young woman would see them and recognize them for what they were. I would grab one at a time and smuggle it into my room and read it over and over again until I really understood what it was all about. I had always assumed that these books were bought and placed there with great care by my mom as a gentle way of informing me about sex, without having to embarrass me with the sex talk. A few years ago, I asked her about it and she laughed. Apparently they were there because she was a teacher and got them from some teacher's book club. There was no careful planning or preparation like I had imagined. They were there simply because she had them and she placed them on the shelf with no hidden agenda whatsoever. She was happy to learn that they provided me with a wealth of information, however, and wished she could've taken some of the credit.

All my friends were virgins. I didn't know anyone who had actually had sex but I and a few friends had gotten close. So I didn't get any advice from friends. I have never been to church and so never received any advice from a religious figure regarding sex or anything else for that matter.

I knew that it was going to happen because it was planned. The two of us and our two best friends were out on a double date on a Friday night. After a movie and dinner we wound up back at my girlfriend's house. We were in her room and we paired off on either side of the bed and began to make out. But it was already late and the boys had to go home. I was spending the night at my girlfriend's house and the boys lived pretty close to one another. So we decided that the four of us would meet up the following morning at one of the boys' houses, since his mom would be gone all day and we would have the house to ourselves. It was settled that we would all go there and all lose our virginity at the house the next day.

When we got to the house, we realized that we had two options. One couple would have to have sex in his parents' bed, or we would have to use the bunk beds in his room. We decided to go for the bunk beds. My boyfriend and I climbed up to the top bunk and our friends took the bottom one. Since we had planned it the evening before, the boys had stopped at a convenience store and bought condoms for us to use.

I was scared the whole time. I remember being very afraid of getting pregnant. That would've been the end of the world for me. And it hurt quite a bit. He was rather large and I kept trying to make myself relax, which only made it worse. But I knew that I wanted to do it, so I just dealt with the pain as best I could. My boyfriend was a little pushy and kept rushing me. After awhile, I just wanted it to end. Our friends on the bottom bunk seemed to fare much better. Apparently she had already had her hymen broken years ago from competitive horseback riding, so it wasn't painful for her at all. I kept thinking there was something wrong with me because they were all enjoying themselves and I was in pain and not having a great time. They were done first and began running around laughing and being silly while we were still struggling to make it happen.

Afterward, I bled a lot. I was in the bathroom for what seemed like a long time. They all kept checking in on me and that made me feel good. I remember that after it was all over he had to go home, so the four of us dropped him off. Then the other couple and I went to get ice cream together. It seemed so stupid, like we were celebrating with ice cream that this big event had taken place. I was still bleeding a bit and was feeling uncomfortable and nervous that my parents would know what I had done when they saw me and the ice cream trip made me sad. I was sad that he had left me so soon after we had sex and I felt like if he had cared about me he would have found a way to stay longer.

The best part was that it was with someone I loved. The worst part was the pain. I really wasn't expecting it to hurt that bad. I was more in love with him afterward than before. I thought that we had shared this special thing and that we were much closer. Afterward we continued to date for awhile. Then we split up, then after high school we dated again for a few years. He was my first love and I am glad that it was with him.

He passed away three months ago. I am still in shock about his death. How do you come to terms with the death of your first love? He was so young and so talented and beautiful. All the things that made me fall in love with him only grew in him with age. He became more talented and more beautiful. I wish that he would've been more generous and loving towards me during our relationship as well as during our first time but I am so happy to know that those things grew in him later on and that he found love before he died.

After the experience, I became more demanding of my sexual pleasure. After having denied myself in order to please him for so long, I realized that I had better learn to speak up or suffer the consequences. When I think about it now that I am older, I just laugh at it all! It seems so funny to me to make a virginity-loss pact with friends and to do it as a group. I wouldn't change it much. I would change the pain part if I could but I wouldn't change the person who I did it with or the company we had at the time. It's a memory that always makes me smile.

The primary advice I would give is to be safe, use protection and don't let anyone talk you into anything you don't feel like you want to do. Approach it in whatever way is best for you but make sure that you are in control and when you decide that it's right, then it probably is.

My father decided that what would "cure" me was to have sex with a woman.

Male: I am 39. I was 18.

I have two stories of how I lost my virginity—one to a woman and one to a man. I was always gay but I up until my late teens I certainly didn't have a word, name, or even understanding of it. All I knew was that I was "different," that the orthodox Jewish religion I had been brought up in abhorred anything even remotely homosexual and that my father was embarrassed by and ashamed of me. It still rankles me now, at the age of nearly forty, to even admit that but nonetheless, it was true. The how and why of how my father knew is a story for another time—just suffice it to say he knew.

My father decided that what would "cure" me was to have sex with a woman. So at my ripe old age of eighteen, Daddy-O contacted my swingin' cool uncle and got him to take me to a bordello in the Hollywood Hills. How did I feel about this? Scared. Angry. Confused. Excited. Bottom line, I wanted him off of my back and this seemed like a pretty interesting way to go about it. Also, you gotta understand that, at the time, I was a very naïve, sheltered, awkward and socially inept individual.

So, my uncle and I arrive and there were three women watching TV. One was probably in her sixties and the other two looked to be in their twenties. We all sat around talkin' shit for a few minutes when the old lady suddenly said, "Okay, which one do you want?" It was really weird to just sit there and choose who I was going to lose my virginity to but what the hell, I chose the brunette!

We went into a bedroom in another part of the house and she took off her clothes and laid down naked. I was SO EMBARRASSED!!! She told me to take off my clothes, which I did, then I laid down on my side next to her and proceeded to go on a non-stop fifteen minute long ramble of everything that would come into my head! Finally, she told me to just chill and she started to feel me up. I started to feel her up too for good measure.

She was pretty, nice body, friendly and she was doing her damndest to get me hard, which was not an easy proposition given the circumstances! Still, I finally got hard and she asked me if I wanted to put a condom on before we did it. And here is where I made a very thoughtless and potentially deadly choice. I decided not to put one on and I remember thinking that if I got AIDS and died that it would serve my father right. How messed up is that?!!! If anyone is reading this and you are going through something/anything similar, do yourself a favor and wear the damn condom! You can process your feelings later; just protect your life now! Anyways, back to the story—so, I'm on my back and she straddles me and slides on down. I don't think you need to hear the mechanics of it all.

> **Throughout the United States, approximately 4% of the population self-identifies as gay, lesbian, or bisexual.**
> - Laumann, Edward O., John H. Gagnon, Robert T. Michael and Stuart Michaels. 1995. Sex in America. New York, NY: Grand Central Publishing.
> Source: www.randomhistory.com

What I do want you to hear is that all I can remember thinking at that moment was about a boy named John who had been my first real love. We were young (seventeen years old) and everything was against us. I hadn't even known until then that I did love him. But I did realize, right at that moment of losing my virginity to this woman, that what I was doing was utterly wrong for me and that I would NEVER "sell my soul" like this again for the rest of my life. I also realized in that moment that I was GAY GAY GAY—and honeys, I ain't never regretted learning that!

So—I bet you're wondering how I lost my virginity to a man! Well, not too long after my experience in the Hollywood Hills Bordello-of-Delights, I left home for good and moved in with some college students in a noisy apartment in Hollywood. I was Y.O.U.N.G. and almost totally inexperienced. Well, wouldn't you know it but Gay Pride was happening that weekend and I met these two hot guys who wanted me to come home with them. Hmmmmmm—so I DID! We chatted for a while, had some wine and then we went into their bedroom.

Now, up until this time I was used to oral sex, sweat and hot and heavy tongue dueling—but I had never even thought about anal sex, it simply wasn't in my repertoire. That was the night I found out about it. It hurt and I cried out from the pain but he kept kissing me and telling me to relax and that it would soon feel a lot better—and he was right! I suddenly felt this wave of pure desire and ecstasy wash over and through me and suddenly in my heart, I knew that I had come home, that this was right for me and that I could at long last stand up and say "I am me, I am Gay and I will forever after this honor MY truth." And I have. It was a wonderful, beautiful, hot, fun, earth-shattering and life-altering moment—and I am forever thankful for it.

***W**hen I was thirteen, my mother sat me down and gave me the dreaded sex talk. She was very open and candid with me. She said at some point in the near future I would be thinking about having sex. I wanted to gag.*

Female: I am 36 now. I was 16 when I lost it. Joe was 18.

I had no specific expectations of how it might be. I didn't have any real romantic notions. I had done some heavy petting and a lot of making out and sex was just a natural progression in my opinion.

Joe was a boy I had been seeing for about five months who could be described at the time as a "death rocker." In modern-day terms he would be "goth." I wasn't punk or goth per se but I wore a lot of black—my mother described me as "punk rock chic."

Joe had another girlfriend. I lived about thirty miles from him and we went to different schools. He had a car. I didn't. I knew about his girlfriend because I met the two of them together. The introduction was by my best friend, Susan, who lived in the same town as Joe. She went to high school with him. He would always tell me he was broken up with her and I chose to believe him... like an idiot. Though I always really knew he was lying.

When I was thirteen, my mother sat me down and gave me the dreaded sex talk. She was very open and candid with me. She said at some point in the near future I would be thinking about having sex. I wanted to gag. She said that when I did, I needed to use protection because there was no way she would put up with having a pregnant teenage daughter. Her advice was not flowery nor did she tell me to wait until I was in love. But she already knew that I had a good head on my shoulders as well as being mildly prudish and she wanted to make sure that I was protected. My father and I never talked about sex—ever.

I didn't hear rumors about sex. Most of my friends had already done it and it was no big deal to them. I know I would ask questions from time to time. I remember telling one friend that Joe put his finger inside of me and I thought that was so dirty. She laughed at me and said that it wasn't a big deal. When she said that, I realized that it really wasn't so bad.

I am not religious and wasn't brought up that way, so no advice there.

I knew Joe and his other girlfriend were having sex and I thought that I could win him by having sex. So I told him I wanted to. He came over to my place and we tried but his penis wouldn't go in. We must have tried for an hour. It was very frustrating for both of us because it never happened. I feared I had become a disappointment to him. About two or three weeks later I decided that I was going to try again.

I planned the whole thing. I told my mother I was spending the night at Susan's house. I called Joe and told him that this was the night. Of course he was available. It was just after Christmas and I had five hundred dollars in Christmas money. Being that he had the car, he drove. When he showed up, there was another girl with him, so we had two extra girls including Sue. Somehow (I don't remember how) we picked up these two punk rock guys to even things out and we were ready to rock. These guys who we picked up were not your garden variety suburban punks; they had nasty reputations. I thought that was scary but also a little cool. The problem was that my money was thirty miles away at home and I was the one who had to foot the bill for the hotel we would be staying in, so off we drove to my house. When I got there, I lucked out, my mother was at work. I grabbed the cash and after two or three tries, we found a seedy motel. By this time we had been drinking some.

The room smelled like a farm. It had one bed with a large closet with no door off to the side. We had all been partying and at some point I decided it was time. So Joe and I moved the big dresser in front of the closet doorway and put a mini-fridge on top. That was as private as we could make it.

I was pretty tipsy when we did it, so I don't remember my thought process too clearly. I know we used a condom. I do remember that it hurt and I derived no personal pleasure at all. It was over in about fifteen minutes and I was grateful to be done.

I don't remember him being thoughtful or respectful. But he did know it was my first time, so he was as gentle as he could be. After we finished, we went back out into the room and continued to drink and party.

The guys went across the street to buy more provisions. My best friend was asking me how it felt. She wanted to see the condom. She was really drunk. I tried to find the condom before she could find it but she won. I remember being slightly embarrassed. I also remember seeing the blood on it. We said "eeewww" a lot and that was pretty much it. I guess I fell asleep soon after and when I woke up early in the morning, the room was a disaster. Sue had thrown up all over the bed, the punk guys peed on the walls and they tore the TV down from the wall. We got out of there fast. Fortunately my name was not involved so I never got in trouble for any of the damage.

Even though the way I lost my virginity was raunchy, I was glad that I crossed over. It was kind of like the first notch on my belt. Not that I wanted or had many partners. But because I played around with the punk rock crowd, I saw it as a fitting punk rock way to lose my virginity.

For me, the best part was that my parents never really gave me a reason to rebel but I did like to hang with the quasi-rebellious crowd. I felt a little like a rebel that night and had a bizarre sense of pride. The best part actually had nothing to do with him at all.

The worst part was that it hurt.

After having sex with him, my feelings for him didn't change. I thought I was in love. I thought that it was a natural progression in what we had already done and I had hoped that he would choose to only be with me after that. HA! No such luck. Now he got to have sex with BOTH of his girlfriends.

I know I told my close girlfriends about it immediately and about a month later I told my mother, who wasn't surprised.

He and I went out and broke up about three times after that in the course of a three year period. Sometime later, when we were in our mid twenties, we saw each other. We lost touch and then found each other on-line and have kept in touch that way ever since.

After losing my virginity, my views on sex didn't really change. The pain that I felt didn't deter me from doing it again with him and the more I did it, the easier it became and the more I liked it with a skilled partner.

I still feel the same way now that I did then. Kind of like looking back with a Cheshire Cat grin on my face. I have never had any regrets about the way I lost it. I wouldn't change a thing. Perhaps it would have been sweeter if I had done it in a more private setting. But overall it's an awkward situation. The girl lays there like a log and waits for it to be over.

My advice to virgins would be to make sure that you are mentally prepared. My decision to have sex was mostly due to the fact I wanted my boyfriend to stop seeing his other girl and only date me. That's not the best reason, not even a good reason but I guess it was the logic of a sixteen year old girl who thought she was in love. I knew in my heart that I was ready though. I knew I wouldn't regret it and I didn't.

Don't have sex because he wants to and you feel pressure. Sex can be great if it's done for the right reason. Only you can decide what the right reasons are for you. But if you confuse sex with love and hope that because you share that side of yourself with a guy he will love you, you might wind up crying yourself to sleep feeling used. If that is the first way you experience sex, it could make a lot of trouble for you later.

I *would later hear she became a mother at seventeen.*

Male: I am 47. I was 13.

I had no idea or expectations whatsoever at that age. The urge and desire to experiment was derived from a Catholic education of "you must be good and sex was bad" and further stimulated by adult magazines I would steal from a barbershop. She was fourteen, a neighbor, very tall girl for her age—about 5'10". We dated in a "youth" sense. I had known her for two months.

My parents gave me absolutely no advice. I think they expected my Catholic upbringing and school to provide that. The only thing I heard from my friends was just that it felt very good and to be sure to pull out in time. Considering I was very young, I was probably the one to be able to give advice rather than hear much of it. Any advice I got from religious sources was just from the nuns in school who told us that sex was a sin and on and on. They brainwashed us with how terrible it was, only causing us to want to explore.

We did it at her house on the sofa. Her parents were working. It was somewhat premeditated. We didn't use any form of birth control, never discussed it, other than pulling out when close to coming to climax.

I was incredibly excited, perhaps the greatest and most exciting feeling up until that time in my life. I was not scared whatsoever. I was very much respectful and sensitive to what she was feeling. She experienced great discomfort but kept encouraging me to continue, telling me she had read it would get easier after each time. The first time we tried it was not successful so we tried again a few hours later and it went in.

Feeling myself inside a girl for the first time was incredible. I recall thinking, "what else could possibly feel this great?" After years of masturbating and thinking about *it*, I might as well have died after that first orgasm from intercourse. There were no bad parts, only a desire to do it again and again.

As much as one could at that age, I felt very close to her and special that she shared that moment with me. The biggest fear was, of course, if she would become pregnant, which would be a monthly worry for the next two years as we continued to have sex and always without birth control. I loved her as much as a fourteen year old could.

I never told anyone until years later when we broke up. I did not want other guys pursuing her, so kept it quiet.

She moved away. I would later hear she became a mother at seventeen. I chose to lose my virginity at that time with that girl because I was young and the opportunity was there. For a boy my age it was like hitting the lottery.

As far as affecting my attitude towards sex, if anything it created more of a need or constant desire to have it. Ironically she was the only girl I had sex with prior to my wife, who I met at age seventeen. Since age thirty-five, while still married to the same woman, I have had many affairs, some that lasted years, some very long distance with little sex involved and are more emotional and since the Internet, MANY quickies. I don't think starting young is the cause of that behavior though.

Even now, when I look back on my first experience, it remains the most special sexual experience of all time in my mind. I would not change it at all.

I believe when you are ready, that is all that matters. As Americans we are unlike other cultures in regards to sexuality. The important thing today is birth control and safe sex. I see little value in the whole "virgin" importance but rather see it important for youth to date many different people for both emotional and physical experience.

I'd just like to add at that young age there was seldom a day over two years that we would not have sex. Ironically it was right after coming home from Catholic school. It was a miracle she never became pregnant.

"Just saying 'no' prevents teenage pregnancy the way 'Have a nice day' cures chronic depression."
- Faye Wattleton
Source: www.emotiquotes.com

I thought that if I went to bed with every man that I liked, then I was somebody to them.

Female: I am 46. I was 22 years old.

I had not a thought in my head on how it would be and it kind of snuck up on me.

He was five years older and my fiancé. We had met at church and I was madly in love with him. We dated about seven months.

My parents gave me almost no advice and my two older sisters have no recollection of advice either. I had only seen a penis twice, once at a nursing home job and another in a magazine. I knew you put one in the other and it could be pleasurable, that's it.

I didn't get any advice from religious figures. Golly no and I went to two years of Bible school after two years of college.

I was renting a room in a house and he lay on his back on my twin bed and I strad-dled him. There was a bit of teasing and when I came down too far, my virginity was gone and a bit of blood told us so. It did not upset me, I remember being sort of proud. As to birth control, I don't recall him "coming" and after that he encouraged me to find out about myself and make an appointment to get the Pill.

It hurt slightly, not at all as much as I thought it would. It didn't worry me and that always puzzled me, because it was a sin to do it before marriage. There was just this feeling of smugness and when I began to bleed the small amount he stopped and I don't remember bleeding that much ever again.

I don't recall at all what his reaction was. I don't think he got in that far the first time. Ever since, I have always considered myself very tight and sometimes have pain at the wrong angle.

I was smug, proud; not of losing it but that we were obligated to go ahead and get married. We decided not to wait two more months for a for-mal wedding and eloped within a couple of weeks.

I really had no one to tell because my whole life revolved around him.

I was one hundred percent naïve. He kept me from my family and friends. He had beaten his first wife and then much less frequently beat me.

We separated after six months for less than a month and afterwards I went back to him. We divorced after a year of marriage.

And what would every woman say, "He was the love of my life." Yeah, right.

Sex quickly became a way to show men who I was. For many years I was very promiscuous, until I realized that it wasn't who I was. That is really the saddest part. I thought that if I went to bed with every man that I liked, then I was somebody to them.

I only can think that he didn't deserve me. My virginity was a precious gift and he got at least two virgins and I have yet to get even one.

My advice to virgins is, make it what you want it. Have it with the one you love or not. I had great sex with that husband. He and I were good in bed, don't get me wrong, yet sex now is a bother and with back injuries and such I would rather not deal with it. I really did not have a brain or thought of my own at even the old age of twenty-two and if I had known myself better then, sex the first time may have had more feeling.

The experience taught me that obsessing over sex only leads to bad things.

Male: I am 23. I was 18.

Honestly, I really had no idea. I just knew that I was tired of being a virgin. I wanted to get it out of the way. I didn't care if I didn't have sex again for years, I just wanted to do it once, just to see what it was like and so that I could say "I'm not a virgin."

I met her in August before my senior year of high school. She was a freshman. We actually met because we were in band together, as lame as that sounds looking back on it. When we met, I was seventeen and she was fourteen—and I feel dirty writing that, because it sounds bad. By the time we did it, it was April, I had turned eighteen and she had turned fifteen. So we'd known each other for six or seven months.

I think to this day, I haven't had a sex talk with either of my parents. It's just something that I've pretty much figured out on my own.

I think I was the second or third guy in my group of friends to lose their virginity, so I didn't really have much to go on. We joked about banging girls but we were all pretty much dumb on the subject. When I was a few years younger in high school, I would hear basically the same stories from the seniors and upperclassmen. They would just talk about "doing" some chick but there was never anything more than that, so I never got any "tips" per se.

I was raised Roman Catholic, no sex before marriage, no "safe sex". I can't even imagine what type of advice a priest would give me.

We did it at my house, in my room, on my bed. My parents were away for the week and I invited her over.

It really was a surprise. The thing is, when we met we hit it off real well. She was very intelligent and very mature for a freshman, so we talked about everything and eventually it led to sex talk. We dis-

144

covered we were both virgins but the twist was, she wasn't sure if she was hetero, so it threw a wrench into the works. Basically, I had a huge crush on her but she said, "Look, I might be gay. I think I am but I'm not sure," so she was kind enough to not want to break my heart but we both had said "Well, let's lose our virginity to each other. We like each other, we respect each other, etc." But she said, "The problem is that you like me a lot and I wouldn't want to turn around after we had sex and say nah, I think I'll stick with girls, because that would be devastating." I agreed with her but said "Please let me just think about whether or not I could handle just having sex for the sake of having sex." So a few days went by and I decided, you know what, I can do this, so I told her I could and she said "Well, I don't think you can, so we're not gonna." I got pretty mad and didn't talk to her for a while and that was pretty much how our friendship was for the next few months. We would be really close, then get into a fight and not talk for a week. A bunch of things happened between us that are sort of relevant but unnecessary in terms of this story. Basically, I invited her over because things with us were not good and I wanted to just have a chance to discuss everything and try to make it all better. When I asked her to come over, I seriously had no intention of having sex with her. It was just in talking, sitting close to each other, touching each other, things started happening and kept happening and kept progressing and finally it all just came together.

We used a condom, that was all.

Like I said, I had had huge fights with this girl, she had hurt me very badly, so part of me was like "Just get off, who cares about her, she broke your heart, just use her," but this other part was "Well, maybe if you're really good, she won't wanna be gay anymore." I don't know what I was thinking but overall I think my heart was just racing and all I could think was, "Don't cum too fast, don't cum too fast, enjoy this, make it last, make it good."

I wasn't sad at all and not really scared. Obviously I was happy but all the things that had gone on between us pretty much filled me with tons of varying emotions. Like I said, I was happy to be having sex but angry at other things; my mind was just spinning.

I think I was respectful and gentle. I wasn't just banging away like crazy. I actually remember that after a short time I felt like I was going to cum, so I stopped and regained my composure because I didn't want my first time to be over that quick. So I settled down, then got back to it. I came, then we cuddled for a bit, then she said, "Want to go for round two?" I swear those were her words. So we went a second time.

Despite her claims of being a lesbian, she was the one who recommended we do it again and obviously I didn't have much experience in hearing girls moan and stuff but the noises she was making and the things she was saying made me feel like she was enjoying it a lot and not just acting for my sake.

I had a little bit of trouble getting it in. She had been with one other guy (which was part of the animosity that had gotten between us) but it had been a while since that happened and I know you didn't want porn descriptions but I'm above average in size (not trying to brag, honest, just giving the story), so it took a bit to work it in.

The best part was that I was losing my virginity to a very attractive girl. The worst part was all the circumstances that had surrounded it and all the crap that had gone on between us in the previous months

Afterwards I was very calm, I guess with a sort of subdued pride. I remember when she left, my thoughts were basically "Holy shit, I just lost my virginity!" I was kind of in a daze the rest of the day/night.

At that time, like I said, there was still part of me that was mad at her for the past but I was hoping that even if I couldn't sway her back to hetero status, at least we could be friends again and that this might've just done something to keep us closer.

I remember the first person I told but I don't remember how soon after it was. It happened over the spring break vacation, so I didn't see most of my friends until about a week later and I just sort of dropped some hints. If people would ask, I would say it but I didn't run around wearing a shirt that said "I lost my virginity!!" or anything.

We had a volatile friendship. We kept talking over that summer. We would hang out in groups, watch movies and stuff. In October of my frosh year of college (so about five or six months after it happened) we got in another big fight and haven't spoken since and I have absolutely no idea where she is now.

Early on, when we were talking about taking each other's virginity, we just felt a mutual attraction. I liked her because she was smarter than even most of the girls my age and we could talk about things, we could debate things. We were on a similar intellectual level and honestly, I just thought she was really hot. I guess she liked me because I treated her well: I didn't talk down to her. I respected her and everything but like I said before, some part of her must've just decided she didn't want to lead me on and in April when it finally happened, I really have no idea. We just started making out, hands went under clothes, clothes came off and it happened.

The experience taught me that obsessing over sex only leads to bad things. If I just relaxed and wasn't so focused on it, I probably could've done it without so much stress and drama surrounding it.

I just look back and think about how for the first three years of high school I had done everything I could to avoid the clichéd relationship drama. I had a girlfriend or two but I still tried to avoid the whole overblown theatrics of high school. Then finally my senior year everything imploded and it sucks, because when I think about losing my virginity, all these other memories come flooding back about the shitty times that led up to it, rather than just thinking about the hot girl that I first had sex with.

All I can say is that I would've liked to have had sex in the September/October area, when we had first met. I wouldn't change the actual act itself, I was happy with that. I wouldn't change the girl, I was happy with her. I would've just changed the circumstances surrounding it.

I honestly have no idea what sort of advice to give. If you wait and wait and wait for the perfect person, you're gonna build it up too much in your head and will probably be disappointed. If you wait to "fall in love," same thing. If you just go to some party and find a slut, you'll probably feel bad about it later. I mean, I can only compare to my situation.

I wish I would have waited.

Female: I am 20. I was 14—twenty days before my fifteenth birthday.

I actually thought it would be like the movies: candles, roses, all that jazz. With someone I loved.

He was one of the most popular guys in my high school. It was the summer before my sophomore year and he was going to be a senior. He pretty much "de-virginized" all of my friends and he was beautiful. I actually knew of him, I really didn't "know" him. I just got up the nerve one night to IM (instant message) him online. And he noticed me after I told him I was interested.

My dad, of course, tried to lock me in the house but I don't think I really had "the talk." My parents just thought that not bringing it up would be the best thing.

My friends all started having sex on a regular basis after they lost their virginity, so I thought it wasn't that bad. After all, all of my friends had better stories than I did!! Ha!

NO advice from religious figures.

I snuck out of my house in the middle of the night and he picked me up down the street so the lights wouldn't bother anyone. He lived in the basement of his family's home, so we really didn't have to be too sneaky. I went there KNOWING I was going to lose my virginity. I went to the mall that day and bought a nice little bra/panty set with my girlfriend. And seriously, sneaking out in the middle of the night–it was inevitable.

I think we used a condom, I am not actually one hundred percent sure! I was not scared, just very apprehensive. When we got inside of the house, we went to the couch and watched TV. After about ten minutes of just sitting there, I told him, "I could be doing this at home" and it was pretty much on from there. I know it sounds as though I was experienced in this field but I actually had never even gotten to second base at the time, I just KNEW I was ready to get it over with and I was so CURIOUS. We did the whole thing. I had never been touched in the area, so when it happened I was in heaven…HA…until it went in. He was on top, my fingernails were well planted in the inside of his thigh, getting harder as he pushed inside me deeper. It really did not feel good at that point. I wanted to tell him to stop and to get back down there and lick a bit more. But I didn't, I went through with it. There were splatters of blood all over the bedding.

He was sweet and gentle, very much so. I mean, he had to be: He was having sex with me and he wanted it too. It was a bit awkward but I really liked him but I knew he thought nothing of me, well not at the time. I guess it was wishful thinking that if I had sex with him he WOULD like me.

Of course he had trouble getting his penis inside of me. Nothing had ever been inside and not to mention his penis was a bit large. (I now know the measuring chart for size.) Ha!

The best part was foreplay. The worst part, trying to sneak back into my house.

Afterward, I felt totally happy. I wanted to call everyone. But I opted to just go to sleep.

I liked him and wanted him to like me (NOPE).

I told all of my girlfriends, most of whom had had sex with him already. So we shared stories! I know it sounds stupid but we were so young.

After we had sex, I went out of state for the summer and found out that he started dating another girl. So that was the end of that. We hooked up again later but it was just to piss off his current girlfriend off (kids are so cruel).

NOW: he probably got fat and knocked some girl up. Ha! I don't know what ever happened to him. I moved to the city to go to college and he was long gone by then.

I chose to lose my virginity with him because I was just ready to experience what it was like—so, so curious. And he was just a hot guy, it could have been anyone! (sad to say.)

It didn't color my attitude toward sex. I started dating a guy that September and stayed with him for a year and a half, so in my mind, the boyfriend took my virginity because I LOVED him.

I wish I would have waited. All I had was a couple more months to find the guy that I ended up loving. DAMN!

My advice to virgins is: I mean, wait if you want, it's better but honestly do young adults really listen to advice that older people give?

***B**oys loved to boast about their conquests and if they could be seemingly uninterested like it was no big deal, it was even better by them.*

Male: I am 38 years old. I was 14.

At the time I really just wanted to try it. The circumstances were fairly unimportant to me. I just wanted to do it with the first girl willing. I had messed around with girls enough by that time that there were no mysteries as to the lay of the land but I had no idea how it was going to feel. I wasn't scared, in fact I was looking forward to it.

The girl was a sleazy heavy metal type. Although she was all into Sabbath, she could play flute like an angel. I was learning a new instrument to fill a needed spot in the orchestra, so she was assigned to work with me during class in a private practice room. She was two years older. We would practice for a while, share a couple of smokes (yes, you could smoke in designated smoking areas of school in those days) and make out in the practice room. I had known her for maybe six months.

My parents were full of hippie values. I was told all about how I should love and share with someone special. My parents were both single for years leading up to this time. The disco era had them both partaking in frequent partners where love had nothing to do with it. I was getting one thing from conversation and another by example.

I don't recall hearing any bad advice from friends. I had heard stories of guys mistreating girls in some sort of apish bang a fist on their chest kind of thing. Boys loved to boast about their conquests and if they could be seemingly uninterested like it was no big deal, it was even better by them. I found that all pretty gross. I did my  share of bragging afterwards but I never spoke poorly of it or her. Keep in mind that this girl and I were far from being boyfriend and girlfriend. We were friends that fooled around. We never swapped notes in the hall, or phone calls after school. There was a different girl that was responsible for stealing most of the virginities in my group of friends. I knew that I didn't want to be the last guy standing but I wasn't going to take the same path, or at least the same girl that they all did.

As far as religious figures, we were hearing that although sex was a good thing, premarital sex was a bad thing. My best friend (still my best friend twenty odd years later) was being raped regularly by a priest in the rectory. Their advice never went far with me.

I invited this girl over to my house. My parents (Mother had recently remarried) were home, probably watching *The Cosby Show*, just downstairs.

I made the invitation with the intention of having sex. My only surprise was that I actually pulled it off.

She was on the pill. STDs were not nearly the issue then that they are today. AIDS hadn't even happened yet. Condoms were a last resort back then.

Fortunately for me, she took control. I was happy that someone was sort of showing me the ropes as opposed to letting me fumble around. I remember my heart going like mad but in a thrilling kind of way. I may have been scared but I would liken it all more to the thrill and scare you get being on a carnival ride. Not the type of fear that had me thinking "what am I doing here?"

It was all very playful. We talked our way though it. I was awkward but she was helpful. She had much more experience and was sharing her knowledge with me. It was not a lovey-dovey experience, although we were deep kissing and fairly passionate. We were pretty silly during it. Neither one of us was too concerned about the implications of sleeping together. There were no rules so long as we kept talking it through. It wasn't like we were asking things like "Can I try this" but more like "That feels good" or "Ouch."

She had as much fun as I did. There was no weirdness about it. She knew I was a virgin and she was having fun teaching me. I think it was equally exiting for her, as it was for me.

We did it a bunch of different ways. She helped me in some of the times but I wasn't having a hard time finding my way around. I did slip out a lot but I wasn't having trouble getting back in.

Best: At one point she took a pair of handcuffs that I had laying around and cuffed me to my brass bed. She did all sorts of wonderful things to me then. She ended up on top of me and allowed me to just be somewhat still and enjoy myself.

Worst: One of my friends knew what was going on. I couldn't contain myself and let the beans spill about what was going to happen. He called in the middle of it all. I didn't want my parents coming upstairs to tell me that I had a phone call while I was naked in bed with a girl, so I dove for the phone. He was asking if we were doing it. I'm going "Yea, like right now."

Instruction in sex is as important as instruction in food; yet not only are our adolescents not taught the physiology of sex but never warned that the strongest sexual attraction may exist between persons so incompatible in tastes and capacities that they could not endure living together for a week much less a lifetime.
~ George Bernard Shaw, Everybody's Political What's What, 1944
Source: www.quotegarden.com

He teased that he was coming over right that minute to mess me up. I had to beg him not to. He was the kind of guy that would have and thought it was hysterical. That was a piece of it all that I could have done without.

I felt great about the whole thing. I learned so much and performed well. I didn't orgasm until we had done it for a couple of hours. I was too wound up to cum. I was feeling proud and like I had taken a step closer to being a man.

I never felt love or romantic connection with her, although I was physically attracted. Maybe that was a good thing because I didn't have the added pressure of her not liking me if I screwed up. I really didn't care if she thought I was terrible. I was a rookie after all. She was cool and sweet and kept it light.

I got together with my friends late that night and told them every last detail. They busted my chops but we were all happy for one another when that time came for each of us.

I actually went twenty years without speaking to her. I had moved to another city and lost touch with many people from my past. I recently came across her email address on a school web site and we have been bullshitting back and forth for about six months. She is on her second marriage and has a child going to the same school where we were going when this all took place.

I lost my virginity at that time with that girl because she was willing and I didn't need to talk her into anything. There was never any conversation about whether I thought she was a slut or if I was going to spend the rest of my life with her because we had done this.

I haven't met a girl yet that was so free and take charge in the bedroom. That's too bad really. I wish women were more comfortable with sex than I have experienced them to be. I would always rather hear a command than a complaint. I have never known two women who like the exact same thing, so guidance is helpful. Phrases like "I like it when you do this, like this" are too few and far between in my opinion. I liked that this girl had no problem expressing that.

It was a great experience. I'm happy about the way it happened for me. Although doing it with someone you love is great, this was a good way to learn before all of that. When I finally did do it with someone I was in love with, it was great that we didn't have to fumble around like two blind mice.

I probably should have done it with her more after that night. I would have been better at it the next time I climbed in bed with a girl.

My advice to virgins is to have fun, be safe and communicate. Don't forget the fun part. If you are going to do it, then you should enjoy it, so don't get all hung up in the meaning of it all. Don't give it up too freely either. Do it with someone you can trust who won't be an asshole after. In turn be decent and respectful yourself. Regret sucks. Be careful! If you are taking a girl's virginity, know going into it that there is the risk it could be unpleasant for her.

I took a girl's virginity my senior year of high school. Without being too graphic, it was very physically painful for both of us. We sort of got stuck together for what seemed like an eternity. It may have only been twenty minutes or so but it was bad. She tightened up so much that I couldn't move and had to wait until I lost my erection to separate. At that age, it wasn't an easy task. She was in obvious agony, crying, whimpering with every breath and it was awful. I have always wished that it had been nicer for her. I had a hard time with it (always hurting the ones you love) and never wanted to try it again with her. We dated for a while longer but I never wanted to go through that again. I took another girl's virginity in college but the hurt there was all mental. I think she saw her virginity as a precursor to marriage. I didn't see it that way and I know it hurt her badly. I never would have done it if I knew that was what was going to happen.

He was very gentle and I did not have an orgasm. He did.

Female: I am 49. I was 17 when I lost my virginity.

My expectations were that I wanted it to be the kind of experience that Romeo and Juliet shared. I'm a true romantic at heart. I was at seventeen and I am still a romantic.

He was my first boyfriend and was twenty-one. I met him at a party that was arranged and he swept me off my feet.

I had known him close to a year.

No advice from parents. They liked him. We didn't talk about it.

No advice from friends either. It was this event that went along with marriage.

The advice I got from religious figures was wait until you are married.

We did it in his parents' huge bed when they were away in Europe. I chose the night. We drank Champagne. It was incredibly romantic. We didn't use birth control.

I was scared but happy. It didn't hurt at all. I did not bleed either. He was very gentle and I did not have an orgasm. He did. He came on my tummy, as we had planned. I was sore afterwards.

He was very respectful, sweet, joyful and it wasn't his first time, so he wasn't awkward.

He had trouble getting it in. We spent hours in foreplay before I let him do it. He was very patient. He would stop whenever I asked him to. Finally it just happened that he was inside.

The best part was the surrendering to each other and the closeness it brought to us. I was happy afterward. I thought that I loved him. Actually we became engaged.

I told my mother.

I broke up with him and went off to college. When I got back, he had married someone else. I don't know where he is now. But at the time, I was really hurt that I lost him. I won't forget him.

I chose to have sex with him because there was some peer pressure. We were going together for a year. I thought that I loved him.

I'd always believed and I still believe that sex is an expression of love. I was naïve and pressured to fit into "Life" and its expectations. I tried to convince myself that I was in love and that I wanted to get married and have children.

I wouldn't change anything. I am what I am because of my experiences.

My advice is make love when YOU feel like it is the right time. Don't give into peer pressure. Learn as much as you can about human sexuality. Talk it over with a therapist. Be aware of your body and its relationship to your mind. We are all unique individuals and we have a unique experience in life that is ours. The more we understand ourselves, especially before we share ourselves with someone else, the more fulfilled we feel with the experience and the more we can truly connect with our beloved.

> *"Credibility is like virginity.*
> *Once you lose it, you can never get it back."*
> *- Unknown*
> *Source: www.quoteparadise.blogspot.com*

Once heard a guy used his gym socks as a condom.

Male: I am 50. I was an "old" 32 when it happened. I was like that movie, *The 40 Year Old Virgin*.

I had no real expectations, just hoping it would happen.

I met her through a friend of a friend, she was about thirty-five and was divorced. I knew her about two or three weeks before we first had sex.

Dad never said much at all. My mom always told me not to do anything. That advice kept me from enjoying myself for years to come.

I heard some extreme rumors, especially in high school. Once heard a guy used his gym socks as a condom.

I wasn't much of a church-goer before that time, so I had no advice from any religious figures.

We did it in her bedroom, after drinking some wine downstairs. Once we had a few drinks things just started heating up. I was surprised at first. We didn't use any birth control.

I know it started slow, kissing etc, then she went upstairs and came back down. She had taken off her panties and bra and then she invited me up to her bedroom. It was a hot summer night. I remember it was stuffy, hot and the room had air conditioning that she finally turned on. Her five-year-old son slept in next bedroom. It made me nervous that he would hear us and wake up. Once she grabbed my penis, that was it. She did a little oral, then we had intercourse.

I might have been too respectful; I think she wanted me to take charge more. Awkward too and I am always sweet.

She said she came right after I did. She had to tell me to stop. I remember her repeating "oh god, oh god."

I had no trouble at all getting it in. She was ready.

The best part was finally doing it but wish I had gone down on her, orally. As for how I felt afterwards, I had a few emotions: regret for not doing it sooner, pride in finally doing it.

Afterwards I wanted to see more of her; I mean dating, etc.

Some friends were told.

We broke up after few weeks. I called to arrange a date one day: She seemed upset that I called her, then I got upset and never called again. Don't know what happened to her.

As for why I lost my virginity with that woman, it seemed like the right thing at that time. She was kind of horny and so was I.

Not until later did my attitude towards sex change. Then I found I was attracted to women and they were to me. For years I had the impression that woman were just teasing me and not really attracted to me.

Now that I'm older, I think back and feel that it was great but wish I knew then what I know now.

My advice to virgins is to just go with the flow. Maybe try different things: positions, toys, etc. Make it an adventure, not a chore. If you find you have problems, get help soon. Don't wait like I did. Now that I am older, I have changed so much.

A dvice from my parents? About homosexuality ??? NONE. About sex in general? NONE. I never had that "talk" with my mother.

Female: I am 47. I was 32 when I had my first gay experience.

I really had no expectations. Had fantasies though. Of course reality never measures up to fantasy so I was probably a little disappointed. She was someone I met thru a personal ad in a local paper (before Internet). She was about eight years older than me.

I knew I was gay at around age twelve. When I was watching the Olympics I saw Olga Korbut, a Russian gymnast, and for some reason (she wasn't particularly attractive!!) I felt something. Then Winter Olympics and Dorothy Hamill (more understandable). I just felt an attraction— something.

As for how my being gay had an impact on my first straight sexual experience (if that's what you are asking), I just was in denial mode. I put it away in a place that I just didn't access. I was in hetero-suburbs-teenager land—no concept of homosexuality involved. I knew no one gay, it wasn't a real concept. So it had no impact except for the fact that I didn't especially enjoy hetero sex. It hurt, I think I bled. Maybe subconsciously because my head wasn't into it as it should have been.

I knew her a very short time. Not sure of the exact time frame. But I think the whole purpose of the relationship was to explore my sexuality, so that being the point, we got right down to it.

Advice from my parents? About homosexuality??? NONE. About sex in general? NONE. I never had that "talk" with my mother.

Advice or rumors from friends—this is kind of a difficult question considering I didn't have any gay friends at the time I had my first lesbian experience. My friends at the time were all straight and we didn't really talk about sex explicitly. The usual innuendo but nothing implicit.

Did I get advice from religious figures? NO!!!! Are you kidding?!?!? If anything the message from religious people was "DON'T DO IT!! It's a sin, blah blah blah."

We did it in her bed in her home. I definitely knew it would happen. Like I said, this was the point. Did I know it would happen at all ? That's different. Probably not. It was kind of an accident. I guess it had to happen, though, eventually. I've always been a procrastinator! I always do what I have to do—eventually.

We didn't use protection. From what??? At this time, AIDS wasn't considered a threat in the lesbian community. We both had no illnesses or diseases. I've never used "protection" with any female partner, other than just knowing her health status.

It was kind of clinical. She talked about it. We both had feelings for each other and I don't think we could have done it if that hadn't been the case. So it was a bit more than clinical but still I felt anxious. It felt great. She went really slow—almost too slow. Telling me what she was going to do and what she wanted me to do. Happy, sad, scared?? Really none of the above. It was just natural. A little tense before the fact. Then relaxed. No fear—that I can recall. Maybe there was a tiny bit of fear that I wouldn't know what to do and make a fool of myself. But no fear as far as going through with it.

I think I was very respectful. I tried to reciprocate but that really wasn't her purpose at the time. I believe I was sweet (hope so), a little awkward probably (hell, it was my first time!) and probably gentle—the first time— later on I tended to be more aggressive but not in a violent way. I guess she was pleased!!! She considered herself to be quite the knowledgeable lesbian, sexually. So I imagine she was quite pleased with herself. She did not want to be penetrated (as most butch women tend to feel) so this wasn't an issue.

The best part obviously was just doing it—finally. Specifically, the best part was when she made me come, by manual penetration—then oral. The worst part was not being able to reciprocate but she convinced me it was okay so I felt okay with it then.

I certainly had no regret. Pride? No, I don't think pride has anything to do with any kind of sex. But I guess I felt relief more than anything else. About myself though—hard to say—just natural.

I think it made us closer romantically. She more than me probably. We both knew from the git-go that sex was the mission but we both felt more attached after the "act".

I didn't tell anyone afterwards. All my friends at the time were straight. Certainly didn't or wouldn't tell family.

She still lives where she did then, I assume. I've seen her once or twice at Gay Pride Festivals. We chatted for a few minutes but that was it. We don't communicate in any way anymore. But there are no hard feelings.

I chose to lose my "virginity" at that time with that person because I had just gotten divorced (from my first and only male partner and father of my two children) so I was starved for attention at the time, any attention. It wasn't even my purpose to seek out gay people. I had picked up the free paper and was reading the personals section and came upon all the different headings and *Women Seeking Women* was one of them! I think my eyes popped out of my head. I had no idea. I read them but felt strange answering one so I put in my own ad. Wish I still had it but it's lost to posterity unfortunately. It would have made an interesting artifact. Anyway, she answered it and we hit it off and discussed the "mission" and we met for dinner and well, the rest is history.

It's hard to say whether it colored how I feel about sex. I think one's attitudes towards sex are inborn. I think one can learn certain things about sex but as far as changing or affecting ones attitude about it—I just don't think so. My first experience was gratifying to me but I've always been a "reciprocator" and since she wouldn't let me at the time, she did later on though, I've always felt that it should be equally and mutually pleasing. I've been that way with both sexes. I think that's a particularly "butch" attitude, not to be reciprocative. Definitely not a straight male thing. So that's an interesting concept, though I realize it's not your objective with this survey.

Now that I'm older I look back on the experience fondly. Amused too. I was so naïve. So unknowledgeable.

I have NO regrets. I would have done things differently in the relationship (I was "bad"). But not with the first sexual encounter.

My advice to virgins is to be explicit about what you want and need. To be relaxed and under no pressure. Try to have some romantic feelings for the other person because it makes it physiologically easier (if you are wet). I think if your mind and heart is into it, then the experience will be a good one. But that's just my point of view.

If possible, try to have your first time with an experienced person. It helps if at least one of you knows what she is doing. Also to have played with toys and/or masturbated to climax, so you know what the expected outcome should be. So you know what it takes to come, so to speak.

I think the dynamics of gay/lesbian sex, at least as a comparative tool, is so different than straight sex and this might make an interesting study in itself.

The whole scene makes me feel like I was used as a meal ticket and a play toy.

Male: I have just turned 65 but feel like I'm 40. I'm planning on surviving until I'm at least 120. I was 20 years old and recently discharged from the Navy.

I expected that losing my virginity would be a big deal. It didn't turn out that way.

She was a girl I met one day on the bus. I was wearing a badge for the Democratic National Convention and she approached me and asked about the convention. She was nineteen. We dated for about two months before we had sex with each other.

My parents always taught me that it was something special and should be saved for my life partner. I guess my juices got control of me and I forgot what I was taught.

It wasn't a subject that my friends and I discussed. Obviously, my shipmates were all sex crazy after each long-term period at sea.

I come from a strong religious background. My grandfather was a priest and my religion teaches abstinence until after marriage.

We did it in my apartment. I didn't know it would happen but things progressed pretty quickly from petting to intercourse. We didn't use any kind of birth control. It all happened so fast that I didn't really know what was happening until it was over. I really didn't think about being sweet or anything else. I was certainly awkward, having had almost no experience, even with advanced foreplay, with this partner. Even so, I didn't have any trouble getting inside of her.

It felt good but was all too brief. Because we had no protection, I was fearful of the consequences. I suppose that I was happy that I finally lost my virginity but I had mixed feelings about what it meant.

The best part was the feeling that I had finally lost my virginity. The worst part was worrying about whether or not she was

pregnant. Afterwards, I condemned myself for not being smarter about using protection.

I felt good about our relationship and the fact that it had progressed to a new level. I didn't tell anyone about it afterwards.

We eventually got married and subsequently divorced. After our first encounter, we got together quite a few times and had sex almost every time. Despite my trying to use condoms, she had a way of dislodging them during intercourse (in hindsight, probably on purpose). After a month or two I broke off the relationship but within a month after that she revealed that she was pregnant and said that it was mine. Feeling guilty and responsible, I agreed to marry her. The day before the wedding, she announced that she'd had a spontaneous miscarriage (unconfirmed by others). Again, feeling guilty, I went ahead with the wedding. Fifteen years later, after she'd had many affairs, I divorced her.

My feeling towards sex remains positive and my new wife and I have had intercourse regularly and have been faithful to each other.

Now that I'm older, I look back and feel I should have waited and made sure that she wasn't using me. The whole scene makes me feel like I was used as a meal ticket and a play toy.

My advice to virgins is to pick your mate more carefully before going so far.

Despite the bad stuff, we had five wonderful children together and when we divorced we agreed on my having custody. My second wife has been a great stepmother and the children all call her Mom.

I *do know all my friends were shocked when they found out I was pregnant.*

Female: I am 28. I was 15.

I had no expectations of what it would be like, not at all. I was very gullible and naïve at that age. He is the man I married. I knew him from some friends of mine. I met him at my fifteenth birthday. He was seventeen. To be quite honest, I had only known him for two weeks, ashamed to say.

My mom talked to me about sex when I was thirteen and she provided me with an over the counter birth control at fifteen but I never told her that we had sex. She found out when I got pregnant by him seven months later.

I really don't remember advice or rumors from friends. I actually think I was the first one of my friends to lose my virginity. I do know all my friends were shocked when they found out I was pregnant. That was totally not like me: the good girl who was honor roll and so on.

No advice from religious figures either. My parents are not big on lecturing us. They don't judge us. They would have been glad if I waited but my parents believe that everything happens for a reason.

We did it at the lake in the back of my boyfriend's truck. I knew it would happen. I provoked it. He says anyway. We used a condom the first time. I was scared, anxious and excited. I had butterflies in my stomach and it hurt like hell. I actually pushed him off of me and said to wait.

I definitely felt more bonded to him afterwards. I felt like I was special to him because he took my virginity and we are the best of friends now.

He was trying to be very gentle but I thought it was very painful. He was definitely respectful towards me before, during and afterwards. He did have trouble getting it in. It was very tight and painful.

The best part was when the condom was lubricated up and wet and the motion of in and out. The worst part was getting it in.

My initial reaction was Oh, my God! I can't believe I just did that.

I felt like he was happy and full of pride. He just took my virginity away from me.

I told my sister afterward. She knew we were having sex for a while. She was up at the lake and had seen us in the back of the truck together. She is older by two years.

I married him five years later. We had our son, who is now twelve.

I chose to lose my virginity with him because I felt like he was my first real boyfriend who was special to me and he was a keeper. I felt in my heart that he wasn't just using me for sex, that he would still be around even if we didn't have sex. He would have waited for me.

I thought sex was a painful situation until we started having more of it.

I am very proud that we have made it work for us. We are going on being married nine years in June and together fourteen years this March. I have no regrets other than maybe I should have waited until I was older than fifteen.

If I were to change anything it would be that I would probably wait until I was older. I believe if a guy really loves you and cares for you he will wait too. If not, then you know they are only in it for one thing and that's not good.

What advice would I give to virgins? To definitely wait. It's not worth losing to just anybody and just because my situation worked out, it doesn't mean that it will work out for everybody. My husband could have easily walked out after the first time and after he found out I was pregnant. Most guys at seventeen wouldn't have hung around. If I had a daughter, I would tell her, like I tell my son, to wait for that special person and just because it worked for me and Dad, it hasn't always been easy. So girls, wait until you have the respect you deserve. Don't just give it up to any guy. It's something we only lose once and we can never get it back once it's gone. So be patient and wait.

"*I know nothing about sex because I was always married.*"
- *Zsa Zsa Gabor*
Source: www.allgreatquotes.com

She had an orgasm and pushed me off before I could finish.

Male: I am 31. I was 15 when I lost my virginity.

I had no idea what to expect. I wanted it to be something romantic that she would remember.

She was a high school sweetheart from a rival school. We met through a mutual friend who I had met on an interschool class trip. The girl I lost my virginity to was fourteen. I had known her for about nine months but we had only dated for a week.

My parents' advice was for me to respect her and to wear a condom. None of my friends had had sex, so they had no advice or rumors to relate to me. I didn't seek any religious advice.

We did it in the basement of my parents' house on the fold-out bed. The whole point of the date that night was to do it. She kept promising me a lingerie party. I was still surprised when it happened.

We used a condom. I remember being very nervous at the time. I had gotten a case of the shivers for almost a half hour and we just lay there, kissing and running our hands over each other's bodies until I calmed down

> *One report states that 48% of women have faked an orgasm at least once in their life. Interestingly, an identical 48% of men also report faking an orgasm at least once.*
> - Durex. "The Global Sex Survey 2005."
> Accessed: December 23, 2008.
> Source: www.randomhistory.com

enough to start anything. I was very happy and very nervous all at the same time. I think that I was sweet, gentle and awkward and I think she was pleasantly surprised by my whole reaction to the situation.

At first she was very tight and just squeezed the tip but then she started moving herself around until she opened up.

The best part was having myself entirely inside of her and having all of the mystery and pressure over with. The worst part was the second time we did it that night. She had an orgasm and pushed me off before I could finish.

I felt pretty good about myself but I still kept thinking about getting the shivers for a half an hour. I felt like I was in love.

I ended up telling my family and friends but not in a bragging sense.

I don't still know her. About two months later she dumped me for a twenty-six year old diabetic she met in the hospital.

I chose that time and that girl because I was in love with her and I wanted to lose my virginity to someone I loved.

As for attitude, I don't think it gave me any attitude regarding sex that I didn't already have.

I still can't believe that my fourteen-year-old girlfriend that I loved and trusted dumped her fifteen-year-old boyfriend for a twenty-six-year-old diabetic she had known for only one day. But still, I wouldn't change anything about my first time.

My advice is that it never seems to get any easier and to always practice safe sex.

*H*e *was respectful and sweet in the beginning. Until I started crying and wanted him to stop, then he was a jerk.*

Female: I am 34. I was 16 when I lost my virginity.

I didn't have any expectations about sex, not that I can remember. I was really scared it was going to hurt.

His name was John and he was seventeen years old; he was my first boyfriend. We had been dating for over a year. I knew him for about four or five years, we grew up in the same neighborhood.

My parents never gave us any advice when it came to sex. They made it clear that we were not supposed to have sex until married and if we did, we were sluts. Men have sex with whores but marry virgins.

Friends would say that the first time was going to be painful and that you would bleed once he "popped your cherry." That there was no way you could get pregnant the first time and that once you've had sex, you would walk different. My favorite: if I didn't have sex for a long time, I would be a virgin again.

We did it at his house, in his bedroom. We ditched school that day. His parents were at work.

We had been talking about having sex. He had been sexually active before with his ex-girlfriend and since we had been dating for over a year, it was time for us to have sex. We pretty much planned the day out.

We didn't use birth control. Since it was going to be my first time, I didn't think I would get pregnant and he said that he would pull out so there would be no way I could get pregnant.

I was so scared and nervous but mostly scared. I wasn't able to sleep the night before. I was so scared my parents would find out. Once I was at his place, I couldn't sit still. He reassured me that everything was going to be all right and that there was no way my parents would find out.

We went into his room and starting making out—he was such a great kisser. Slowly he started to unbutton my blouse, then went to remove my bra. I totally freaked out and asked him not to remove my bra. I was so embarrassed and insecure about my body: I didn't want him to see me naked. I kept my bra on, got in his bed, went under the blankets and then removed my shorts and underwear. I made him turn the lights off and close the curtains so the room would be dark. He took his clothes off and I freaked even more when I saw his penis. I thought it was huge and there was no way it was going to fit inside me. He got in bed with me, we started making out again, then he rolled on top of me. He kept professing his love and how it wouldn't hurt. He then placed his penis in the opening of my vagina. I just laid there: stone stiff, scared, nervous, wondering what the hell I was doing. Once his penis began to enter my vagina, I remember I gasped for air. I started to cry. It was so painful I felt like my insides were on fire.

There was nothing enjoyable about it. I kept crying and asked him to stop. He kept saying it was okay, that the pain would go away and that he wasn't even inside me all the way. He wouldn't stop, he kept going—telling me to relax, that I was making the pain worse by being so tense. I kept crying and screaming that it hurt and for him to stop. He then stated that he couldn't stop just yet because he was about to cum. A couple seconds later he got off me. I grabbed my clothes from the floor and ran to the bathroom. I was in so much pain that it made me sick to my stomach. I stayed in the bathroom for what seemed like a long time, throwing up and crying. I then cleaned myself up, put my clothes back on and went home. All the way home I kept praying that my mom wouldn't notice anything different about me.

He was respectful and sweet in the beginning. Until I started crying and wanted him to stop, then he was a jerk.

He did have trouble getting his penis inside of me. I remember him saying I was too dry and tight.

The best part was when it was over and the worst part was having no control and the pain. I was so ashamed of what I did. For a long time I felt dirty and regretted the whole thing. I hated him, I couldn't bear to look at him.

I told my best friend at the time, Dorothy.

A couple of years later he got a girl he was dating pregnant. They had a boy but didn't stay together. From what I've heard he's a great dad, very devoted to his son. He still lives at home with his parents and works at a local restaurant as a bartender. For whatever crazy reason, he never learned how to drive and takes the bus. FYI—We had a fifteen year class reunion several years ago and he came up in conversation.

I thought I was in love with him; a year of dating at that age seemed like a long time. So, I caved in to the pressure.

That experience left a very negative view towards sex and men. For so long I was so ashamed, angry, disgusted with myself and others. I blamed myself for what happened and had serious trust issues with any man I attempted to date. In my mid-twenties I sought professional help.

Looking back, I can't believe how naïve I was. If I had it to do all over, I would change the person I had sex with and I would wait until after high school.

My advice to virgins is to be very careful and always use protection. You may have a choice when it comes to pregnancy but not STDs or HIV. Talk to an adult you trust about sex; what their experience was like, do they regret anything etc.

We slept the whole night together but it was as if we were repulsed by our closeness.

Male: I am 46 years old. I was 20.

I didn't have any expectation of this event and I had no notion of how I wanted it to be.

I lost my virginity to a woman named Cathy, a mutual friend of a male friend. She was twenty-four. I had known her for about six months. We went to the house she was living in at the time. We both knew it was going to happen. It was sort of pre-arranged.

I was working as a dishwasher in a diner. Cathy came in and sent me a very suggestive note using food references. I replied in the same manner. My male friend and Cathy had just had a conversation about me and my asexual nature. So her come-on did take me by surprise.

She put in her diaphragm. I didn't use a rubber. I was a little nervous but she did a good job making it very relaxed and romantic. I would say I was respectful. I pleased her initially as best I could and then we had intercourse. It was very gentle and sweet. She was very much in control of the situation and was enjoying herself. Insertion was no problem but there was some pain during the act. She mentioned how there was a thin line between pain and pleasure.

The best part was experiencing different positions with her and feeling very close to her. The worst part was the physical and emotional separation we experienced after the lovemaking. We slept the whole night together but it was as if we were repulsed by our closeness.

I did feel good about achieving this milestone. It was good to finally experience sex. I was more or less expected to report to my friend and two other female friends we had at the time. I had trouble communicating my feelings and resorted to reciting a short journal entry, which included the line "My dick hurts."

She went on to marry an older man and raise a family in northern New England. I have long since fallen out of touch.

It's a very quaint and cherished memory. I am glad to have it. There was nothing I would change about the way it happened except maybe, instead of this being a

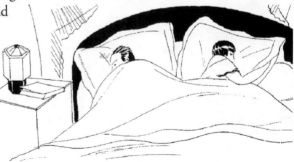

pre-arranged thing, I would've been more proactive and pursued this event with more initiative on my part and not having my first sexual partner know, at least initially, that I was a virgin.

I didn't really get much advice from my parents. In my teen years, my mother "threw the book at me," which meant I got a technical rendering of the birds and the bees. My father took the more sleazy approach and introduced me to the "ladies of the night." This was not carried out to fruition but it definitely "colored my world" of sex.

My advice to virgins would be to take it slow and make sure you have some emotional connection with your first sexual partner. The other thing I would like to add is although sex is important, it's not that important. It really shouldn't be the basis of all interaction with the opposite sex.

I *think that it attaches you so deeply to another person that if you aren't careful you can demolish the other person.*

Female: I am 31. I was almost 20 and was in my second year of college.

I think by this time I was really curious. I had heard everything, seen sex all around me in the media and I was at college where everyone was a lot freer about their sexuality. I guess I expected it to be romantic and mind blowing at the same time.

He was a really good friend of mine in high school. We never dated but he was always around, coming over, we would watch movies together. We started dating my freshman year in college. So I guess I knew him for three years before we started dating.

Advice from parents was not to do anything until I was married. I guess the old standard. Actually, my mom is a nurse and she went into detail and explained everything but I was terribly shy about my sexuality and asked for a book that I could read myself. I grew up in the Bible belt in the South and a lot of sexual talk wasn't as open as today. Also, my grandmother lived with us, which added an even more old-fashioned approach to how I felt about the subject myself. But when I was ready, I told my mom that I thought I needed to be protected and we went to the doctor.

I didn't really get advice from friends. I was very adamant about wanting to abstain. All my friends were active but very protective of me. So I heard nothing of their experiences. I would hear things like: oh this person did it but nothing that wasn't high school. A friend had to have an abortion and that was an ordeal and another girl got pregnant in seventh grade. It just made me want to keep my values and not have to deal with all that.

No advice from religious figures either—although it was ingrained in us that it was a sin.

We did it at this girl's house where we went and stayed the weekend. We were on break from school and were with another couple we went out with a lot. Her parents were out of town and we all made dinner and had drinks and watched movies.

Actually, I had a talk with the girl that night and she asked if we were ever going to and I said no. I was still standing by my guns. I think that I just got so curious about what it was all about. I wanted to know and I thought I was completely in love with this person

"I didn't lose my virginity until I was 18 The first time was a nightmare. Who shows you how to use a condom?"
- *Adam Ant*
Source: www.brainyquote.com

Yes, we used birth control—the golden rule. We used a rubber—is that what they are called?

I just remember the dark and it was warm and he was so loving and really happy. It looked like he was going to explode from the inside out. I couldn't believe that I was doing this but it didn't feel wrong and I trusted him completely. I felt happy and a little more grown up.

I wouldn't change anything where I am concerned. I think that it was a natural progression in my life. I wasn't pressured or scared or trying to hold on to someone. I had been broken up with, told that I was childish, that they were madly in love with me—oh about every excuse in the book and still all they wanted was sex. It is something I had to do on my own terms. But the downside is, I think that it attaches you so deeply to another person that if you aren't careful you can demolish the other person. This guy, when we broke up, called in the middle of the night and said he was going to kill himself and just did a list of other things. It was really hard for him and a lot had to do with that type of intimacy.

It is your life and your body. Always remember that and make the best decisions for you. Live it on your terms and don't worry what friends or boyfriends have to tell you. Just don't rush into something until you are one hundred percent ready and by all means protect yourself. Always.

I *was kissing her goodbye when she asked, "Do you want* *to do it?" I had no idea what she was talking about, so I* *said "Do what?"*

Male: I am 35. I was 16.

It was completely unexpected. I didn't even have a girlfriend at the time, so I had given it no thought.

I was on vacation. My friend Mick went with me and we were walking about, speaking in British accents. Mick knew a girl in the area and she met up with him. The two of them went off to be alone. So, all by myself, walking through the town, speaking with a fake accent, I walked up to a girl and asked her, "Like to go to a movie?" To my surprise, she said yes. She was sixteen as well and worked near the theatre. I didn't see much of the movie, as a lot of kissing was more interesting. I can't even recall what movie it was.

Afterward, I walked her to the parking garage where her car was parked. I was kissing her goodbye when she asked, "Do you want to do it?" I had no idea what she was talking about, so I said "Do what?" She laughed and started taking off her top. "Oh! That!" I said. I had only known her for about two hours.

I'm tall and her car was not very large and we did it in the back seat. That made it uncomfortable, if not awkward. She had obviously done this sort of thing before and was quite comfortable with it. I wasn't sure at all what I was doing but she led me through it and I had no trouble getting it in. She was in charge, so I would have to say that I was respectful. I was nervous and probably a little awkward too. I used a condom.

As for what was going through my mind, there were a lot of things. "Is this really it? Who is this girl? Are all girls this easy? Am I doing this right? Is it supposed to be over already?"

She instigated it. And afterward, she was nice. Kissed me goodnight and then drove away as if it were no big deal. I never saw or heard from her again after that night.

Honestly, it was over so fast there really wasn't a best or worst part. She was a very good kisser. Maybe that was the best part. I thought she was cute. She seemed nice enough. I suppose I have a little bit of regret, years afterward especially. I wish that I had actually known my first.

After it was over I walked away, met up with Mick, who was leaving his girl, and told him what had happened. At first he didn't believe me but by the time we had walked back to the hotel, he was convinced.

As far as advice goes, my parents never gave me advice about sex. They raised me to use my judgment and do the right thing in all matters, sex included but we never spoke specifically about sex. Mick bragged a lot about sex and collected Catholic uniform skirts from the girls he had slept with but there wasn't any advice or rumors. I'm not religious and so never got any advice from religious figures.

I chose to lose my virginity with that girl because she asked and I was so surprised that I was literally in the act before I questioned it.

I'm not sure what my attitudes would have been toward sex if I had lost my virginity to someone else. I think that I'm a lot more picky than some of my friends. I have no desire to just go out and sleep with random strangers like they do. Maybe that was how it changed me. I started off on that note and moved on. They started off sleeping with someone they knew really well and went the other way.

Looking back, I wish that I had waited to sleep with a girl that I actually knew and wanted to be with.

My advice to virgins is don't sleep with a stranger. Find someone you really care about. And, for the guys, think about something else: baseball, work, anything. And don't complain about condoms. Not only do they prevent unwanted pregnancies, they also make you last longer.

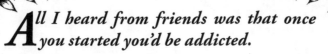

All I heard from friends was that once you started you'd be addicted.

Female: I am 21 years old. I was 16.

I wanted to wait until marriage

His name was Brian. I met him at the mall. He was seventeen years old. I'd known him for nine months before I chose to sleep with him.

I didn't get any advice from parents, they never knew. My family just expected me to wait for marriage; sex before marriage wasn't allowed.

All I heard from friends was that once you started you'd be addicted.

We did it in my best friend's brother's bed. It wasn't planned. We used a condom.

I remember it hurt like hell and I was scared. I was scared that something would go wrong and that my family would find out and be disappointed in me. I was mad at myself for going through with it.

He was gentle and lost like me, for it was his first time too–kind of awkward. He did have a little trouble getting it in but he managed.

There was really no best part. Afterward I had no specific feeling about it, just confusion. My feelings for him didn't change. I thought I loved him.

I didn't tell anyone about it afterward. It was my little secret.

We broke up and I don't talk to him anymore by choice.

I decided to lose my virginity at that time because I felt pressure, not by him but pressure from my so-called best friend at the time.

After that I didn't have sex again for a year. I wish I would have waited. It wouldn't have been him. I wasn't sure about him and would have rather it been someone I could have remained friends with.

Before you decide to lose your virginity, give it time. Don't do it because of pressure, do it because you feel you're ready.

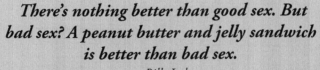

There's nothing better than good sex. But bad sex? A peanut butter and jelly sandwich is better than bad sex.

– Billy Joel
Source: www.allgreatquotes.com

I was a Nervous Nelly. I had no idea what to do and I didn't want to look like an idiot.

Male: I'm 26. At the time I was a sophomore in college, 20, I think.

I had no idea of how it would happen or what my reaction would be. At that point in my life I was more concerned with just doing it rather than it being "perfect". For me, it kind of just happened and then it was over. Somewhat anti-climactic but I was more satisfied knowing that I had finally done it.

She was a girl I met on spring break. She was kind of a party girl but she was really sweet and just loved to hang out. We hooked up over spring break and then it continued once we got back to school. She was a year older than I was but friendly with a few people who lived in our building. I had known her for maybe a month—it wasn't that long.

Advice from my parents? Ha! My parents didn't give me any advice. The one time my mom tried to talk about sex with me was when I was nine years old. She said, "Do you know about the birds and the bees?" I said yes and that was the end of the conversation.

Basically, my one friend kept on telling me not to look at her vagina while doing it because I'd be a shoo-in to bust within thirty seconds. He would also tell me to think about something else so that I wouldn't pop too early. Other than that, the only advice I retained was from watching pornos and seeing how the pros did it.

I had no advice from any religious figures.

We did it in her bed. I really had no idea it was going to happen. We were drinking in a friend's apartment and somehow ended up back in her bedroom making out. The next thing I knew, we were both naked and I was on top, kissing her. She looked at me and said, "Do you want to do it?" I'll never forget what her face looked like. She was so cute and her eyes were kind of glassy because of the booze. I don't think I said anything and just started going at it.

We didn't use any birth control, not a condom or a pill, which was probably a dumb thing.

I was a Nervous Nelly. I had no idea what to do and I didn't want to look like an idiot. She didn't know that I had never done it before either and I didn't want her all freaked out. To think back on it, I wish it was something a little more memorable but whatever—I made it! It felt awesome and there is no better compliment to a guy than seeing a girl squirm in pleasure due to the fact that you are giving it to her good. It was strange to see this girl that I liked react in such a pleasurable way but it was a huge confidence builder, knowing that I could please her.

I was happy, scared, sad, all of it. It all happened so fast, so all of the emotions were pouring out of me at the same time. I was respectful and gentle and sweet. I mean, how do you think I was able to do it in the first place? Remember, she was the one who mentioned it and I just went ahead with it.

Her reaction was great. She was as into it as I was. From what I remember, I'm sure that I probably had to guide myself in and make sure I was going in the right place. I didn't want to hurt her, so I went in easily. She prepared herself first and then I came in.

The best part was finally accomplishing it. At that moment I felt like I could move forward with my life. I was "in like" with her and felt that she should be a part of it too. The worst part was it was all over too quickly. As an inexperienced person, it didn't last more than five minutes. I wish I could have gone longer but hey, it was my first time.

I felt great—no regrets. I wish I could have opened her head to see how she felt but I guess that is all part of the game. I liked her. She was exactly my type: short, cute, blonde hair, fun to hang out with and her body was amazing. I liked her before then and after having sex with her, I was starting to fall in love with her.

I told everyone! I didn't send out a mass email but I think I made a few phone calls to my home friends and just let the people at school gradually find out. It was a very important moment and people need to know about this!

I still know her. Being that she was my first, I still have strong feelings for her. We are hot and cold these days and it saddens me. We had a great relationship but it was in school and we were both so immature. Now I'm realizing that I messed up things with her and really want to try it again but she's hard to get in touch with. Whenever we do see each other, it usually ends up in us hooking up and I'd like for that to be more but for some reason she's hiding from me.

Losing my virginity wasn't really a choice. I wasn't saving myself for anyone. It was the type of thing that just happened and I went along with it. I liked her and she liked me and it made perfect sense. That night it was unexpected but it turned into a relationship.

I think the experience colored my attitudes towards sex a little bit. Having sex on a regular basis definitely helped me along, as it would anyone else.

Now that I'm older, I look back and realize I was so dumb when it happened. I was just a young adult, trying to party like a normal college kid and meet girls at any chance I could get. I was really lucky to be with this one girl. She's awesome.

If I had it to do over I'd use protection, for obvious reasons. From talking with her over spring break and getting to know her a bit, she explained how she was only with one other person before me. Did I believe her? To a point but at the same time she's not the type of girl to run around town spreading her legs to random people.

My advice to virgins is to masturbate once before you actually do it. It'll give you more time when you are with her and save yourself the embarrassment of the one pump chump.

All I thought was oh my God! I'm having sex for the first time with my boyfriend's best friend.

Female: I am 34. I was 19.

I don't think I thought about it much.

His name was Bill, he was my boyfriend's best friend. I think he was twenty or twenty-one. I'd known him about a year or so.

My parents did not talk about it—ever. My mother is afraid of it and my dad just didn't talk to me about it.

From friends I'd heard it was painful/so great/horrible/doesn't last long/not what they had expected.

I had no religious advice. Never—didn't and still don't care about what any organization has to say about what I want or don't want to do.

We did it in my boyfriend's bed. It was a surprise, because he had a girlfriend who was out and my boyfriend was at a party and we were drinking a little and it just sort of happened. I don't believe we used birth control.

All I thought was oh my God! I'm having sex for the first time with my boyfriend's best friend. I'm a total bitch—but let's get this over with. It wasn't good or romantic; just kind of like okay, done!

He was very nice to me—before and after. We remained friends—like it didn't really happen. I know it was not his first time and he didn't know it was mine.

Yes, of course he had trouble getting it in.

The best part was right before it happened. We had a really nice night of just hanging out. They were having a party and he was "keeping an eye on me"—whoops! He was always very nice and cute. The worst part was when my boyfriend came back. He just kind of knew and that sucked!

After losing my virginity, I felt hungry—very hungry and like I didn't want to do that again anytime soon.

I still liked him as a friend.

I told a couple friends.

I'm sure he eventually got married. I know he got a little chubby. I don't still know him.

I didn't choose it, it chose me. We were both just kind of there. I know I wasn't particularly interested in doing it again—it wasn't that great. I wish I had done it with the boyfriend instead. I bet we would have gotten married. He even asked me three years later but I didn't want to move out of state. Nice guy! I would have only changed the person.

Like I told my niece, don't have sex while you are in high school. There is more than enough drama there to deal with, no need to add sex!

I felt like a very lucky boy.

Male: I am 38. I was 12.

I had no expectation, as it just seemed to have happened. She was the girl my mom got to watch my younger brother and I when she worked late. She had sat for us many times. She was eighteen. I had only known her a few hours all told. She had maybe sat for us four times in a four-month period.

My parents never told me anything about sex except that it should always be a positive experience. My friends and I were all young. We were jerking off to *Penthouse* forum letters. There was no religion in my household.

We did it on the living room floor, then the couch and then my mother's bed. I had no idea that we would have sex. I was the new kid in town everyone beat up and picked on because we were different.

We didn't use birth control and I did cum inside her many times that night.

It all started with me giving her a back rub while she laid on the floor. I started with her shoulders through her shirt and her back for a bit. After a while she lifted up her shirt and let me touch her skin. She was not wearing a bra and I could feel the side of her breasts. She was a curvy girl with large breasts. I was very happy and getting aroused. After a bit she asked me to rub her legs. As I did she started to tell me where to put my hands. Soon my hands where in her crotch and she was rubbing herself through her pants. She was very warm and her pants started to feel moist.

I did what she asked me and when she got up, I thought it was over until she took off her pants and taught me how to give her oral sex. I must have started too gentle because she kept forcing my face deeper into her wetness. I think she had cum a few times at this point. She took my pants off and slid me into her very easily.

The best part was how it felt like her pussy was milking me, better than any masturbation I had ever done. The worst part was cumming inside of her. I was freaked out but she

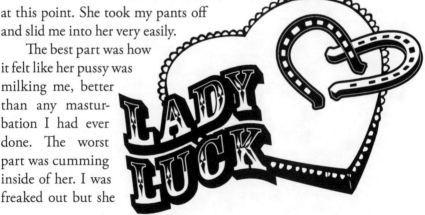

said it was OK and we would do it more.

I felt like a very lucky boy. She taught me lot about sex as long as I kept it a big secret.

I didn't tell anyone afterwards, not until I had moved.

I have no idea where she is or what she does.

It really wasn't a choice on my part. She was the one who chose to do it and I went along.

That experience did color my attitude towards sex. It was great. I have become very sexually active in my life and I have always loved to give oral to a woman because of how she taught me and how much she loved it.

I may have been too young but I had fun. I wish I knew then what I know now. We would have never stopped.

The only advice I have for virgins is this: it is just sex. Have fun.

My mother...would tell me to imagine that Jesus was in the backseat...and that would stop me. What really stopped me was imagining my mother in the backseat.

Female: I am 49 yrs. old. I was 22 when I lost my virginity.

I was one of the last of my friends to do so.

I had a good feeling about sex and wanted it to feel natural. I had come close before but had always stopped before anything happened.

He was a fireman I met in church. He was also a singer. He was singing in a church production and I was impressed. He was twenty-five when we met. We saw each other for about a month before we made love. We went out, stayed in, dated.

My mother always said to wait until I was married. She would tell me to imagine that Jesus was in the backseat with my date and I when we were together, so that if we started something, that would stop me. What really stopped me was imagining my mother in the backseat. My father seemed to make it clear, without really saying anything, that sex was a good, natural thing and something that should be enjoyed between two people who loved each other.

My friends were all supportive of me losing my virginity but only if and when it felt right. They made it clear that there was nothing wrong with me for still having my virginity and their only advice was to be sure it felt right to me.

No religious advice, not really. Except for the party line the church gives out that it is a sin to have sex before marriage. I don't think I ever really bought that though. I think that was partly because of my dad's attitude.

We were in my apartment, in my bedroom, making out. We had done that before but he had always stopped us because he knew I was a virgin and he didn't want me to regret how I lost my virginity. I wanted it to happen. When he stopped us because he was getting beyond being able to control, I told him not to stop, that I was ready and that I wanted to have sex with him. He asked me if I was sure and I said yes.

We didn't use birth control but he did not cum inside me, for what that's worth. I thought it was worth a lot. It wasn't. I ended up getting pregnant. Luckily I miscarried, so I didn't have to make any further decisions.

I loved the feelings. Of course, the initial tear of the hymen hurt a bit but the feelings that happened before and after were amazing. I had never felt anything like it.

I was very happy and not scared at all.

He was very gentle and very sweet. He was very mindful of the fact that this was my first time and no one else would have that. I don't remember him having any trouble getting it in at all. He was not a virgin, although I don't think he was terribly experienced.

The best part was the feeling of closeness when he first entered me. I still love that feeling of initial penetration. There is something amazing about feeling filled up that way. The worst part was when he came out of me.

I had a little guilt, I think. I was glad I had done it and that it was with this man but my upbringing made it impossible not to have a little bit of guilt. I convinced myself I loved him. I didn't. I liked him a lot. I enjoyed his company and I was very attracted to him. And I felt safe with him.

I told my best girlfriend afterwards.

We stopped seeing each other shortly after we had sex. He went back to his former girlfriend, got engaged and married her. I did tell him about the pregnancy because I thought he should know but I only told him after I had miscarried. I heard from him years later because he and his wife were not able to conceive and he was convinced that was his "punishment" from God for having taken my virginity. I had to see him to tell him how much bullshit that was and that I had no regrets about having had him as my first.

I haven't seen him in twenty years.

It felt right. I felt safe and I knew he would be gentle and respectful. I think it may be one of the reasons I love sex. I didn't have sex for a while afterwards because of the scare of pregnancy but the next time I had a boyfriend, we did have sex, naturally, and it was a lot of fun. I got on the pill before so I didn't have to worry about pregnancy and at the time, that was the only thing we really worried about.

Looking back, I feel very warm and good about it. I just wish he didn't think he was punished because of it. I have no regrets.

I would change one thing. When I was in Germany, the summer before that, I almost had sex with someone who was and is still one of my best friends. I wish he had been my first just because of who he is. But I'm not sorry it happened the way it did.

Wait until you are ready and until you know the man/boy you are with values what is happening. Don't be pressured into having sex because "everyone else is doing it" but when you truly feel you are ready, enter into it with openness and enjoy the sensations.

I do love sex. I love just about everything about sex. I love the feelings and the smells and sights. I wish we could realize how wonderful sex is and not attach so much value judgment to why and when people have sex. It is a wonderful thing when shared by two consenting, caring adults.

This was 1981 and the biggest fear about sex was pregnancy and possibly herpes but there was no fear of dying, unless you feared your parents like I feared my dad.

Male: I am 41. I was 16.

I definitely had expectations. I was a senior in high school and had heard many stories from friends about getting laid. I was raised Roman Catholic, so there was always a struggle in my mind between sex after marriage versus sex before. Many of my friends were having the same struggle but still went through with it when the chance arose.

She was seventeen and a high school senior with me. She had moved into the area the year before and one of my friends had slept with her before. She had a reputation for being loose, which was a real downer for me but she and I always flirted with each other and really had fun kidding around. My sixth hour class was next door to hers, so we always walked from lunch to the classrooms together, exchanging sexual innuendos with flirtations the entire way. I knew her about a year when it happened.

My parents were very Catholic and of Irish descent. Pre-marital sex was forbidden and it was very black and white. No question about whether or not you should. It was an absolute no.

As for my friends, from a guy's perspective, sex was cool. And that means any kind of sex. If you got laid, you were cool. If you got oral sex, you were cool. And the fact that you experienced it made you a cool person. This was 1981 and the biggest fear about sex was pregnancy and possibly herpes but there was no fear of dying, unless you feared your parents like I feared my dad.

I went to a Catholic grammar school and

went to confession sometimes. The priests would tell us to abstain but all of us found that unwarranted because they never had done it themselves. So there was not much value in what they said.

We did it in the front seat of my dad's '77 Ford LTD. I played football and we had been talking about going to our school's soccer game, which was played on Thursday nights. I had a grammar school friend that had been killed in a car crash, so I went to that wake after football practice, then went to pick her up, then to the soccer game.

I had absolutely no clue it would happen but once we left the soccer game and I was taking her home, it was clear she wanted to do it and I didn't want to say no. There would have been too much risk that it would get out to my friends that I wouldn't do it, so we pulled over in a quiet neighborhood and started right there. I was surprised because the further I went, she wasn't stopping me as all previous girls had, so I just kept on going. And we went all the way.

With regard to birth control, I have to laugh. There wasn't much access to any in 1981. You could go to a gas station and buy a condom from a bathroom dispenser but that was about it. And I wasn't going to do that.

I was elated, sad, scared, happy and many other emotions all at once. Here I was, finally becoming a man, yet it was in my dad's front seat. Would he know it in the morning? Would she get pregnant? Would she enjoy it? I had no idea what I was doing and it showed when I blew it in her. That really scared me and I realized later she probably was on the pill because she slept around a lot.

I was definitely respectful of her but when we were done I was pretty embarrassed. The surroundings were bad. I was doing something that was totally against everything I was told growing up and I really didn't know this girl very well, let alone the possibility of getting her pregnant. So I tried to act like it was something that I did all the time and just got dressed, started up the car and took her home.

She seemed a little awkward afterwards. I think she was used to being with many experienced guys and that wasn't me.

I had absolutely no trouble getting it in. I think she may have even had a baby before she moved into town and that was a reason she moved from a neighboring state. There was more than enough room to get in and out.

The best part was getting the whole first experience behind me and being able to move forward. The worst part was the guilt around the Catholic opinion that you shouldn't have pre-marital sex. There was definitely regret because she was not close to me and there was not going to be much after that. And there wasn't.

I thought that she was loose, she was easy and I didn't have any respect for her at all after awhile. She just really became a tramp that was sleeping around a bunch and it took away from the entire experience.

A few of my friends talked about it and then I started realizing that she was doing it with one of them. He was an extended friend; more of a friend of a friend but it still reduced or removed any respect I had for her.

I haven't seen her since high school graduation, over twenty-four years ago.

It was circumstances more than anything that made me decide to lose my virginity with her. She happened to be there with me and she was very willing to do it. I was ready to do it and would have done it even with another girl, so it wasn't the girl as much as the circumstances.

I didn't have sex for another year and was not one to sleep around a bunch. If it was a girl I liked and we both wanted to, I'd have it but I definitely did not go out and get sex like Charlie Sheen or Wilt Chamberlain.

Now that I'm older, I definitely wish I had waited for a better girl, or even for the one I ultimately married. It was an experience that I would repeat but do feel that it shouldn't have happened because of the risk of pregnancy. I never would have been able to stay with her long term, so I'm glad nothing happened from a pregnancy standpoint.

I wouldn't change anything about the experience. I'm not a believer in that theory. I made my choices based upon where I was at that time and what I wanted at that time, so I don't have any regrets and don't think that way.

My advice to virgins is to wait until you care about someone. You don't have to wait until marriage but at least care about the person. Then once you have lost it, enjoy it.

It hurt but not as much as I expected. It didn't feel that great.

Female: I am 26 years old. I was 18 years old then—a second semester freshman at an Ivy League university.

He was also eighteen, closer to nineteen and was an engineering freshman. We were friends. I can't remember how we met. We lived in the same dorm. I lived on the top floor and rarely left my room until second semester. He lived on the floor below me. Neither of us were part of the social crowd. We were engineering students, so we were part of the engineering crowd. There were nine of us—five boys and four girls. We all drank together and partied together.

Looking back, I guess there was an attraction between us. There was definitely sexual tension. We constantly wrestled playfully. He would attack me outside or in his room. We put holes in walls, broke garbage cans. Our physical interactions comforted me.

One night he came over. I can't remember why. It could have been after a party. I was asleep or going to sleep and there was a knock at the door. The rest is a blur. I can't remember if we were talking before or what. I know that we started to wrestle. And he tried taking off my shirt and I tried taking off his clothing. Before I knew it, his pants were down and we were silently contemplating having sex. I think I dared him! The scene was not very romantic—it was my dorm room, small and private. We were on the floor in between my refrigerator and my bed.

The actual sex wasn't that romantic either. It hurt but not as much as I expected. It didn't feel that great. He was not compassionate at all—no hugging, kissing, comforting. But he was respectful. I was very distant. I didn't try to kiss or hug him. I just looked at him, trying to understand what was going on. Emotionally, I didn't feel anything. There was no intimacy and I didn't care. I didn't know enough to care.

Afterwards he got up. And I remember being afraid to ask him where he was going because I thought he was leaving. I finally did in almost a whisper. He told me "the bathroom to clean up."

Afterwards we sat Indian style on the floor in the spot where we had just had sex. There really wasn't much to say. We tried to figure out what to do next. I went on the offensive. I told him that I didn't want a relationship. In truth, I did like him and I did want a relationship: I was just afraid of being vulnerable.

From that point on, things weren't the same. I blame myself for that. I changed. I became distant. I acted like it didn't happen. He became best friends with my best friend—which caused extreme tension.

Our junior year, we finally talked about it. He apologized. I apologized. To this day, we don't speak directly but through our mutual friend. I haven't seen him in years.

We used condoms. I knew nothing about them. He educated me from that point on. I never went on the Pill.

The best part was being that physically close to someone. The worst part was when he left.

Afterwards I was numb but not in a bad way. I just didn't know what to feel. I didn't know who to tell. It didn't seem like a big deal. I was the only virgin of my friends. My friends all did it with their boyfriends. I did it with a friend. I was ashamed because I couldn't call him my boyfriend. I was not his girlfriend. But I didn't feel as though I made a mistake. It was very odd.

Prior to that, my knowledge of sex was extremely limited. I took a sex education class in high school but didn't pay attention because I wasn't sexually active. It wasn't something talked about at home. My dad never discussed it. The one time I told my mother that I wanted to remain a virgin until marriage, she frowned. She didn't want me to have an unsatisfying sex life in marriage. I told my mother that I lost it about year later. I needed comfort and she was just very distant. It was almost as if she didn't want to pry. I never told my father, I think he just assumes so.

I attended Catholic school for twelve years. That very much shaped my attitude. Sex was for procreation and only procreation. Any type of contraception was sinful and masturbation was sinful as well.

I don't think the experience colored my attitude. I was distant before him and still am. If anything, it highlighted my issues with intimacy.

When I look back, I feel that person was young and inexperienced. I had no business having sex but I wouldn't change actually having sex then. The knowledge that I have now is a direct result of my experiences. I would change how I dealt with it. I would have been truthful about my feelings for him. Before actually having sex, I would have stopped to ask "is this something we really want to do?" I would have kept it between us. Not telling my friends, etc. It was private and should have remained so. Advice....

I would tell virgins that there isn't an age limit you can put on losing your virginity. It has nothing to do with age. It is all about your emotional state. One should be ready for the emotional consequences and attachments that come along with being intimate. I was eighteen and I was WAY too young. At twenty-six, I barely feel old enough to have sex. I do feel that I can handle the potential outcomes—good or bad. I also realize that virginity isn't a moral issue. It's a personal one. A decision made by you. No religion or religious figure can make that decision for you. The only way that you will be confident in your decision is if you make it yourself. Plus, you should protect yourself. Research safe sex yourself, don't let anyone tell you. You find out. It is your body. Know what's going in, know what to keep out. You are in control. It has to be done on your terms.

The worst part was thinking for the next three weeks that I was going to be a father.

Male: I am 45. I was 16.

I had no idea what to expect, I just heard from my friends how great it is (like we really knew at age 16!!) She was the girl who lived at the corner of my block. I'd seen her for years and we were the same age. I went to the Catholic school and she was in the public school so we never really got a chance to meet until the summer of '76, when I just approached her and started to talk. We went out about one week before we had sex the first time.

My parents never really talked to me about sex. I had to find out about it like everyone else I knew—on my own. In my group of friends there was one guy who was about four years older than I was. When he was in high school he got set up with a girl. He went to her home (no one was there) and they eventually had sex on the couch. He came back the next day and explained to all us "inexperienced" boys exactly how a man makes love to a woman, describing every detail as he relived his experience to a male audience. Looking back at this, I see the humor in a young man who has finally gotten his chance to be with a woman and now thinks he knows exactly how it is supposed to be done.

As for advice from religious figures, I was in Catholic schools for twelve years. Sex is something that was NEVER brought up

We did it in my parents' basement. We were both standing up and she was leaning against a pole. I was nervous and thought she was too because it was supposed to be her first time. She kept telling me that she was my "little virgin." As I entered her I remained still, just moving my lips as we kissed. After a good minute she asked me, "Well, aren't you going to pump?" I had no idea I was supposed to and I didn't know how she knew. Several neighborhood boys told me later that they all had experienced her many, many times.

We had been planning this event for a few days so I did know it was going to happen but I just didn't know how to do it correctly. I was happy, of course. I was now a "man." But I had absolutely no idea what in the world

I was doing. When I finally released it was an incredible feeling. I finally climaxed with the assistance of a female companion instead of being all by myself.

At that point in my life I didn't even know what birth control was. However, for the next three weeks she told me that she was pregnant because she was not getting her period. I still remember the look on her face as I was walking home from school and passing her house. She saw me and ran to her front porch and screamed "I GOT IT!" That was the greatest relief of my life!

I guess awkward was the best way to describe how I was. Especially after the first day we got together. We were in the alley making out and I was trying to give her a hickey. I'd seen them and I figured it was no problem giving one. "OUCH" she screamed, "Are you biting me????" I didn't know a hickey was created by sucking, not biting. It was always awkward with her because everything I did was done for the first time in my life and I never had instructions.

She was helpful to me. She would guide every movement I needed to make. I just thought she was intelligent in that field, never knowing that she had much experience. I had no trouble getting it in. None at all. It glided inside smoothly. It was nothing I had done, I know that. I was just up and in. She must have been excited enough to get moist all on her own.

The absolute best part was the "explosion." I remember removing myself at that point so I wouldn't do so inside of her. Almost thirty years later and I can still see the amount of fluid being sprayed all over the basement floor. More than I have ever produced on my own. The throbbing just continued and was very powerful. The worst part was thinking for the next three weeks that I was going to be a father. I remember my schoolwork going downhill (I was a sophomore) and still remember having a conversation with a classmate about my predicament. It was three of the roughest weeks in my life.

I was picked on a lot as a kid (especially in grade school) and a bit introverted at that time. Afterwards I felt like I had accomplished something almost as a right of passage. I felt my male peers would no longer look down on me because I completed what every teenage boy sets out to do.

Within the first week of dating we used the "love" word every fifteen minutes and were making plans to be married (even before we had sex). It must be because it was the first time in my life a female gave me any close attention. It felt good.

Did I tell anyone afterward? Are you kidding? I told EVERYONE. It was an accomplishment. The Right of Passage I mentioned before means nothing if she and I were the only ones who knew. Besides, I found out many other boys spent time with her and I couldn't let them know I was dating her and not having sex.

Once she discovered that she was not pregnant, I re-evaluated things. I realized it was a close call and could have gone either way. I decided to cool things off and we parted. We still lived close to each other and saw each other on occasion but no hard feelings. I eventually moved from the neighborhood and never saw her again. I do think of her from time to time. You never forget your first!

I'm not sure I chose her. It was opportunity. She was actually my first girlfriend, she was available for it and I allowed it to happen. There was nothing "special" about her being the one. I was young and wanted to experience sex, she was cute and willing.

My attitude towards sex wasn't colored by my first experience. I'd say it was definitely colored by an experience I had several years later. I was twenty-two and got a job right out of college. I had been dating the same girl (not the one I have been talking about) for a few years and never thought of being with anyone else at the time. I met another woman at work who kept hitting on me. I would explain that I had a girlfriend and that didn't stop her. We would flirt back and forth but I thought it was just innocent. She lived alone and told me that I could call her anytime. Jokingly I told her I usually didn't get home until 2:00 am. I was told, that's okay, call me anyway. One early morning I decided to take her up on that and I did call at 2:00 am. I was invited over and brought a bottle of wine. Eventually we had a small affair even though she knew I had another girlfriend. That was when I realized that woman enjoy having sex just as much as men do and there are those woman who will have it anytime with any man, with the same wild disregard to it as men have. Before that I thought all women were straight and narrow, faithful and had morals. I learned at that point in my life just how powerful sex really is.

Looking back on it, first of all I am grateful to God Almighty that I was not a father at that early age. With that aside, I really am happy about it. I learned a few details that day. I also think that it helped me over the next several years to know and understand about birth control. From that point on in my sex-life I have been very careful (and had a vasectomy at age thirty-three). I also look back and see how freeing sex is and try to use those thoughts to guide my children (three daughters and two step-daughters) to see sex in a different light than purely physical. That it is a responsibility and physical is only 25% of the act. Emotional is the other 75%.

I wouldn't change a bit of it. It was totally wrong and not what sex was meant to be but without that experience I would have nothing to compare it to. I don't know that the one experience is what changed the way I act but I have learned throughout the years that (and here is the advice to virgins) one should never feel pressured to do ANYTHING with their own body, especially sex. The inner pressure of wanting this feeling will always be there but the maturity level to understand what you are doing isn't. There is a major difference between having sex and making love. Having sex is cheap—making love is giving of yourself to a special person you have a deep connection with. All in all, making love even feels better physically!

I *was raised in an extremely conservative and religious family and so there was an immense amount of guilt associated with premarital sex.*

Female: I am 35 now. I was 17 then and it was the summer before my senior year of high school.

I grew up in the country, so there was never much for teens to do and certainly no place for them to go. I think I expected fireworks and remember thinking, "is this what everyone rants and raves about?" I wanted the fireworks, that's for sure and it wasn't until many partners later and well in to my twenties that I started to enjoy sex. But I think with age I was able to let go of the religious guilt and standards my parents held us to.

I was very much in love with the boy (love from a teenage perspective of course, more like infatuation I think). His parents owned a summer cottage on the same road as ours and so we were both a part of the young contingency on the road that hung out in their boats and bathing suits all day. He had a crush on me for a couple of years but I was more in to this older boy who looked like the blonde Ken doll. You know—teenage stuff.

A couple of years passed and I noticed Joe growing up (he was a couple of years  younger than I). He had taught himself how to play the guitar and started playing at our nightly campfires and on the dock while I laid out in the sun. He had a dark complexion and would get very tan. I was becoming smitten. It was probably all the classic love songs from the 60s he was singing—James Taylor, CSN, America. I fell hard and fast.

He had been sexually active already so there was some pressure but I don't remember feeling pressured. I was raised in an extremely conservative and religious family and so there was an immense amount of guilt associated with premarital sex. However, it was never anything my parents talked about. I found a book on my pillow when I turned eleven called *You Are Now Eleven* that explained the birds & the bees. I knew NOTHING!

I remember really wanting to do it with him. Many, if not all, of my close friends had already had sex (again—not much to do in the country) and I was very much swayed by what I saw anyone else my age doing.

We did it in the back of my mom's car. We had touched and kissed a lot prior to this but I was very self-conscious about my body, as I had very large breasts, so it was always in the dark. The night it happened I don't remember consciously deciding to lose my virginity. I do remember each step of him pulling up my dress and unzipping his pants and then all of sudden thinking "OH MY GOD—I'm doing it!!!" and realizing, with some sadness, that my first time was now behind me. He wasn't very well endowed so it didn't hurt and there was no bleeding (thank god—since it was my mom's car!) It was soon into it that my mom yelled out the front door for me to come home. We, of course, froze and I was CONVINCED she knew I was in the car having sex. After staying frozen long enough to think she had gone back inside I pushed him off and we sneaked out of the car.

I climbed in to bed that night with an enormous amount of guilt that I still subconsciously carry with me. I am one of six cousins and none of the family ever talked about sex or even made sexual comments or told sexual jokes. Once my cousins started getting married and having children, the social talk and jokes loosened immensely. However, being the only single one, I'm convinced they still temper their talk when I'm around. And it still gets avoided like the plague with my parents. For example, I was flying home recently, overslept and missed my flight and my mother said, "Well why didn't Alex (current boyfriend) call and wake you up?" I'm thinking, "Because he was laying next to me oversleeping too!" Sex is something only done in wedlock.

Anyway, Joe and I were together for almost a year and we continued to have sex. I never received real physical pleasure from it but it felt nice to be that close to someone. That was the best part—being that physically close to someone. The worst part was the guilt in feeling I was doing something very wrong.

He was affectionate towards me and truly cared about me. It was always quick because we were usually sneaking it somewhere. I always felt like I was going to get in trouble or caught. We used condoms (after the first time, which was without protection but ended before he had completed).

I told my close girlfriends but not many people. My mindset was that once I had done it I had lost my excuse or explanation to say no anymore. I became very sexually active in college and learned most of my knowledge while playing drinking games with the girls in my dorm—e.g. orgasms, positions, oral sex, etc.

Joe and I crossed paths for a few years after that but we haven't seen each other in many years. I have heard through mutual friends that he is married with a child. I would love to have an opportunity to talk to him.

I am not one that carries many regrets, as I believe all your choices bring you to where you are currently and removing any of them would create a different reality for you. I remember him and my time with him fondly. I do wish I had waited until I was a bit older and was more confident and knowledgeable. But it was what it was and it is my story. I think

> ### *Why should we take advice on sex from the pope?*
> ### *If he knows anything about it, he shouldn't!*
> *– George Bernard Shaw*
> *Source: www.allgreatquotes.com*

I would encourage virgins to wait as long as they possibly can. I think age brings experience, wisdom and confidence, which can only enhance an experience.

I agree that it is an important part to a relationship. But it's not everything.

Male: I am 24 years old. I was 21. (Yeah, rare these days that someone loses it this late right?)

Honestly, I expected that I would last longer but from the research I have read, the first time is normally the quickest, for there is a lot of uncertainty and discomfort as well as inexperience.

She was a year older than me, a Caucasian gal whom I met through a mutual acquaintance. I am of Asian descent by the way. I knew her for about four months or so. (We chatted on and off over the phone and Internet.) But personally, we met for about three or four dates before we slept together.

My parents would not want to hear about my sex life. Don't forget, I'm Asian, our parents are very conservative. However my aunt injected some education in us when I was in my late teens. She told me to always use condoms. And thus, I've never had unprotected sex. This carried on to my later college years when I took courses about health and diseases, where I was reassured that sex should always be conducted in a safe manner unless you are aiming for a child. Furthermore, I am very opinionated on this topic. So many single mothers out there. I feel bad for them but have no sympathy. I do not believe that a child should go through life without both parents, for that will hinder them in terms of their education due to the bias of the single parent who is raising them. They (the parents) should have been responsible in the first place and not confuse the definition of the words "lust" over "love." But of course I'm getting a little off track here so I'll stop.

Honestly, I am not one to listen to my friends. But after I was de-virginized, I realized that it was not all that great. I mean, I agree that it is an important part to a relationship. But it's not everything. Advice that I did hear was to change up positions every now and then to prolong the orgasms.

I am agnostic, so there was no religious advice.

We did it in my bed. It was really spontaneous and I wasn't sure what to expect. It somewhat took me by surprise but then she whispered in my ear, "I can't resist any longer."

I always use condoms. I make an extra attempt to stop and go buy some if there is a situation where I don't have them. There have been many times where she said that she didn't like condoms, for they take away some of the sensation.

It really felt great. I could feel my muscles tensing and relaxing. Kind of like that psychological theory of systematic desensitization.

I was semi-scared for fear I wasn't doing it right. I had the impression that she had done it before because she was older than me and seemed to know what positions she liked. So I kept asking her if she was okay during the middle of it when it should have been the other way around.

I was showing her that I knew what I was doing. I thought that I did. I started off gentle, of course, and affectionate. Kissing her here and there. Then there were times when she asked for a certain "adjective" and so I then proceeded to go at an aggressive rate.

She enjoyed it but was mad afterwards. It was weird. She wanted me to lie with her for a bit but all I could think about was jumping in the shower and getting ready for work. So she was mad at me for a few days.

This is so embarrassing but at first I was kind of aiming too high (in the missionary position). I took an anatomy course and found out that the vaginal orifice is actually pretty close to the anus. So I realized that I missed too far up, for I feared that I would poke in the wrong hole.

This is probably an obvious question since you are asking a guy. The best part was the immediate moments leading to and after orgasm. The worst was like thirty seconds after the orgasm and afterwards, when a guy feels worn out and incapable of continuing. But in actuality, it's our re-productive system that needs time to recover, NOT our energy system, although it may seem that way.

Afterward I felt just plain ol' good. No regrets. Happy to get my foot in the door, so to speak.

I thanked her! What an awful thing to do after I realized what I said. Thanking someone almost seems as if I paid her for sex or something. She asked me, "What, are you not going to see me again?" I retracted my statement.

I didn't tell anyone immediately afterward. But a few days later I told my one of my best friends.

I still know her but sadly we hate each other now. Well, at least I know I hate her. I am convinced that she used me for money, if not the "lust" part that I was discussing earlier. She never loved me, in my opinion. I try to ignore her. I cherished the times we had. All the romantic nights we had. Camping trips, star gazing on an island out in the bay, etc. She didn't appreciate that it seems.

She got interested in a friend of mine about six months after we dated. I told her that's great. (Sarcastically of course). She says we should still be friends. I say the hell with that. First off, she would not even have met him if she had not met me. So once again I have been used. I think I'm going to start seeing Asian girls from now on. Unless someone can convince me that there are some Caucasians who have a proper head on their shoulders and can be interested in only one guy at a time.

I lost my virginity with her because she kind of forced it upon me. Honestly. I think our third date was a little too early. We probably would have eventually lost it with one another at some point however. The timing part was just not right in my opinion, however the setting was right. In my room. Cold night, under some warm and cozy covers.

The experience didn't change the way I view sex. I am a very educated individual with a different personality than most guys. My feelings have always been the same about sex. There is always a place and time and feeling for it. I'm not like most stereotypical prep boys who are always saying "dude" all the time and strutting their hard-core style and trying to make out with any girl on any given night at the bar. I pick and choose my poison, so to speak.

I don't regret the experience. Like anything in life that involves passion and emotion, when you are in the heat of the moment, you won't stop. The only thing that I do regret was meeting that girl. She was oh so deceiving. But you live, you learn.

I would change the person I was with. There are more things that constitute good sex. It is the compatibility with the person afterwards.

Despite what people say, use protection. I am not here to condemn sexual intercourse. It is huge in our society these days. We can't hide from this social phenomenon. We just have to embrace it and educate ourselves on how to perform it to the best and safest ways we know how.

He fell out once or twice, which is something I was never told about before actually experiencing it.

Female: I am 21. I was 20.

The relationship I had before John was with a woman, so I didn't have the chance to lose my virginity. She and I had had sex but oral sex was oral sex.

John knew that I was a virgin and I knew that he loved sex. He was very sweet about it and while we talked about having sex, he never pressured me. We decided we wouldn't even think about it until we had both gotten tested for STDs. We tested negative and while we had both been talking about the day we would know, now we were faced with whether or not to have sex. I loved him and he loved me; it was just a matter of me being ready for it. I had had oral with other guys and other girls; it wasn't like I was inexperienced or even nervous. I just didn't want it to be weird. The day we got our results, we went back to my place (he had a roommate) and started making out. We had even bought condoms in preparation. In the end, we decided not to have sex because I felt there was too much pressure and it wasn't something I wanted to plan like that.

Just a decade ago, only 25% of women reported experiencing orgasm as a result of intercourse. In recent years, this number has risen to about 45%. In contrast, over 80% of women report experiencing orgasm though oral sex.
- *Kanner, Bernice. 2005. Are You Normal About Sex, Love and Relationships? La Vergne, TN: Lightning Source, Inc.*
Source: www.randomhistory.com

It was a few weeks later, again at my place, in the middle of the day. We were done with our classes for the day and the weather was beautiful, putting us both in a great mood. We were naked and had been kissing and suddenly I stopped and looked at him and said "John, let's have sex." He smiled. "Are you sure?" I smiled back and nodded. He asked that I tell him if I wanted to stop and he got a condom. It didn't hurt at all and I hadn't expected it to. Mostly I think I was amazed at how smooth a penis was, compared to the thrusting fingers I was used to. He fell out once or twice, which is something I was never told about before actually experiencing it. I was a bit confused and wondered if I was doing something wrong. So then I got on top. And then I came. We came together. Oh my God, I still can't believe I came the first time I had sex. We snuggled after, lying on my bed in the fresh daylight coming through my windows. I looked at him skeptically: "So? Is that it??" It took him a few moments to understand I was joking (probably I shouldn't have said it, even though it was funny after).

We were going to his parents' house that night. I remember my constant smile on the train ride over, him asking, "What are you thinking about??" Me, "What do you think I'm thinking about?" Smiling.

It is August now. When I had sex with a guy for the first time, it was seven months ago, shortly before my twenty-first birthday. I was a junior in college. I had heard it would probably hurt but I doubted it would for me because I had discovered I am a bit stretchy, if you will. So I didn't expect it to hurt and because of that, I knew it would be even more painful if it actually did. I just didn't want to finish and then regret what happened. Mostly I think I just wanted it to feel good all around.

We met our freshman year in college, so I think we knew each other for two years but we hadn't really been in consistent contact until the start of junior year. He quickly became my best friend those first two months before we started dating and because we lived just around the corner from each other, we became very close very soon. I kissed him for the first time in late October, the night the Red Sox won the World Series.

I certainly did not consult my parents about having sex, although I'm sure they would have been more than okay talking about it. I grew up in the kind of family where we discussed anything and everything at the dinner table. I learned about sex when I was little. My sister taught me how to read when I was four and I remember finding a book in my room called *Where Did I Come From?* and I read it. I was too young to be immature about it, so I just accepted it and moved on. I also remember coming home one night when I was sixteen from a conference on sexuality with lots of free things, including a Chinese take-out box filled with condoms. My Dad saw the carton and said "Is that rice? You're not supposed to have food in your room." And I said "Don't worry, Dad, it's just condoms." He was relieved and I thought it was hilarious. So I knew my parents just wanted me to be safe and informed. We never really talked in depth about it.

As far as religious views, I went to a retreat on the topic when I was fourteen, I think. I learned that sex is viewed as a holy, blessed thing and that the male should allow the female to climax first. I also learned that you aren't supposed to do so much as to hold hands before you are married, because holding hands leads to kissing which leads to etc. etc. I took the first lesson to heart and threw the rest out the window.

I was one of the last of my friends to lose my virginity. In fact, most of my friends didn't even believe I was a virgin because I was so open with my sexuality. I had been warned against faking an orgasm (which I never did anyway) and warned that it would probably hurt. But then it will be really good! Really. Good. Like a roller coaster?? I used to joke. I didn't tell them when I finally had sex but they figured it out on their own pretty soon after. John and I are still dating and I still love sex.

My advice to virgins is to not rush into things. Your virginity is only as important as you make it. I don't think you should have sex with the first guy willing (I'd imagine if that's how anxious you were, you'd no longer be a virgin) but I don't necessarily recommend waiting until you are married either. John and I were in love and we were very comfortable with each other and that was the best way for me to do it: It might be different for you.

I knew there was something going on with me since I was very little. Probably from age four or so I liked playing with boys, not just for the recreational aspect but because I developed crushes on my friends.

Male: I'm 32. I was 18.

I didn't really have any expectations. I sort of knew that losing your virginity was a big deal from watching movies like *Fast Times at Ridgemont High* but being gay AND male, it was a completely different ballgame! And really, there was no book to help me out or the Internet to look stuff up. I remember going to the library and secretly reading books about sexuality and stuff but even that wasn't much help. Learning the word coitus was hardly any friggin' assistance. But looking back, I guess I did want my experience to be romantic. I will be honest, I was pretty naïve even at eighteen, so I did not really know what to expect. I had fooled around with guys at camp and at home with friends but nothing more than the usual stuff.

He was dreamy, man. He was twenty-two or twenty-three, tall, Swedish (but raised in Boston) and so mature. I met him at youth group for gay teens and he instantly surrounded me like a shark about to attack. For all my naiveté, I knew he liked me. I guess we hung out at the youth group a few times and we eventually chatted about going to a movie. He was really slick and could definitely tell I was nervous. He complimented me on my eyes and told me that I had a cute smile. I mean, anyone will fall for that at eighteen.

> *There is nothing wrong with going to bed with someone of your own sex. People should be very free with sex, they should draw the line at goats.*
>
> *- Elton John*
> *Source: www.thinkexist.com*

I knew there was something going on with me since I was very little. Probably from age four or so I liked playing with boys, not just for the recreational aspect but because I developed crushes on my friends. As I mentioned above, I fooled around with boys from a really young age. I had a buddy named Jim that lived on the same street and we would walk home from school together. A few times, we would go to the backyard of my apartment building and show each other our "things!" I don't remember having any idea what any of it meant but I knew I enjoyed hanging out with him and I guess he was my first crush. At the same time, I knew it was probably a wrong thing to do. I also had a buddy named Sheri who also lived on the same street. She and I hung out one time in the front hallway of my apartment building and I remember her asking me to play doctor or show and tell. She showed me her privates and I was mortified. Not only was I not interested, I was also too shy to show her mine! She got upset and I really knew that it was not something I wanted to pursue. Now had it been Jim, it would have been a different story.

I knew Bob for about a month before we had sex. But we never really hung out outside of the youth group. I guess I really did not know him at all.

My parents did not talk about sex. I'm not saying they are prudes but growing up as a Latin American Catholic boy, you don't get much advice other than "don't ask," "that's not for you to know about" and the old standby "sinner!" When I was about fifteen or sixteen my dad bought me some condoms because he noticed I'd been hanging out with a few girls here and there and he just wanted me to be prepared. He was nervous, I was embarrassed and the rest is history. I'm pretty sure he knew or suspected I was gay but like any other father, at least he took some precaution. Needless to say, I did not use the condoms other than to try them on by myself to get a feel for what the hell a condom felt and looked like.

From my friends I heard the usual type stuff. That the man puts his thingy in the woman's hole and that he then puts sperm in there. Mind you, I had no idea what any of this meant. I first heard this in Catholic school. I find it funny that I learned a few things about sex in Catholic school when really, they are trying their damnedest to shield you from that type of information. They included: the word virgin. I learned all about smoking and tried my first cig in the schoolyard. My friend Melissa told me that the condoms I found in my parents drawer were for sex. (I really thought they were balloons!) I heard the word *lezzie* and yet had no idea what it meant.

From the religious figures in my life, I did not receive any advice other than thinking dirty thoughts was bad and that people waited till marriage to have sex.

Bob and I did it at his apartment. I knew something was up when he invited me back to his place. In fact, at one point, he asked me if I was a virgin. Of course I said no! And you know what? I really did not know I was going to have sex (I hoped anyway) but I was so naïve. I do remember wearing some cool clothes and putting on some cologne beforehand!

No condoms were used. He didn't ask and I did not know enough to ask.

I remember being really nervous. Once we went to Bob's house after renting movies and buying some beers, I knew I was gonna have sex. But of course, I was also quite horny and quite excited. I remember we rented *Chucky II* or something. It really should have been a scary disaster.

Ha! Was I respectful? I didn't know what I was doing! He was slick but also very nice and definitely took the time to romance me, he held me, kissed my neck and chest, he even commented on my cologne (Polo). He was sweet but I'm sure he had an agenda. At one point he asked me if I was sure I wasn't a virgin. I answered with a "no" but I don't think that he was convinced. Regardless, he forged ahead with his plan to seduce and conquer me!!

Trouble getting it in? Yes. It was VERY funny. He was huge and mind you, I did not know what the hell I was doing. I didn't know the concept behind anal sex, I swear! It didn't hurt that much but honestly, it was not all that enjoyable. I didn't do it again for years afterwards.

I guess the entire encounter was the best part. But at the time, the worst part was the fact that I didn't enjoy it too much.

I didn't feel regret but I did feel some shame afterwards. I remember going to visit a friend of mine later that day and feeling so many things and yet I couldn't tell her because at that point in my life I was not out to anyone. And so losing my virginity was my own secret.

I liked Bob but I was unsure of how to be around him after that. I guess I felt ashamed and seeing him only made it worse. I don't think I saw him more than few times after that.

I didn't tell anyone about it afterwards.

I heard he ended up becoming infected with HIV but that was hearsay from other friends who also attended the youth group. So I really don't know what happened to Bob.

I didn't really choose the person or the time. I guess he chose me and he didn't really know I was a virgin. Or maybe he did? Maybe he smelled the confusion in me. Maybe he totally knew what he was doing. Again, I felt that Bob was very slick and very seductive.

That experience did affect the way I viewed sex. I didn't feel that I liked anal sex after that. And at that time, AIDS was such a crisis (and don't get me wrong. It still is). I couldn't get away from billboards and commercials and programs on MTV about HIV. AIDS was everywhere. I didn't feel that putting myself at risk was something I wanted to do. I didn't have anal sex until I was twenty-one and living on the west coast and I met some cute DJ at a club who also seduced me!!

It's like anything else in my life. I have moved on. I don't think it was a negative experience at all. In fact, I really liked Bob and he definitely helped me come out of my shell.

I would do it again but I would definitely do a little more research on gay male sex. I was always such a curious kid, looking things up in the library and stuff. I guess I would have chatted with a counselor or something from the GLBT youth group as well. But what's done is done.

My advice to virgins is to do some research and not to feel pressure to have sex. Although it was cool for me, I would not push it for anyone else. Also, condoms are of such importance, especially for gay men and straight women. But even lesbians need to take precautions. EVERYONE needs to think things through. Pulling out is NOT a method of birth control. Currently, I work for a small school and I am amazed at how misinformed the students are about sex and birth control. I guess the next piece of advice would be for people to get to know their bodies. Read up on orgasms, get to know how your body functions during arousal, I'm serious! It all seems like too much but trust me, your body will thank you for it. I have, over time, learned all about the way my body works, all about the prostate and especially all about condoms and safe sex. It's not as easy as just putting on a condom; you really need to convince yourself that your health should come first.

Enjoy it when it happens, take your time. It is definitely NOT like you have seen in the movies. I guarantee if you ask most people, losing their virginity was not all romance and satin sheets. Besides, who sleeps on satin sheets? YUCK!

My parents NEVER spoke of any of it with me, which was a huge mistake on their part.

Female: I am 36 years old. I was 14.

I have never talked about it so openly. Nor did I ever write about it. I only had it in my head that I should wait. Not for any particular reason. My parents NEVER spoke of any of it with me, which was a huge mistake on their part. But I was so in love and wanted so much to bring him closer to me. It was not planned at all.

My expectations? Not sure, I had always heard that it hurt. AND that if he had an orgasm even NEAR you, that you could get pregnant. Very uneducated about it all.

His name was Hank. We were in high school together. He was a junior and I was a freshman. He was a rock and roller guy in a band, played the bass, had a tattoo. And my parents, of course, hated him. But I loved him so.

I remember my father saying once to me "If you are ever pregnant, drunk or high, don't bother coming home, just keep walking." Yup, he actually said it. It was in a moment of jest. Because they were too uncomfort-able to talk to me about sex. He was kidding at the moment and I knew it but it always stuck with me.

The only thing I heard from friends was that if he came even close to or outside your vagina, it could sneak its way in and you could get pregnant.

No advice from religious figures either. I was Protestant and we didn't have all the sin and guilt stuff. But I did know that the Catholics were guilty about it.

We had skipped school on a warm, sunny June day. We were with about ten or twelve other kids at a house one of them lived in. His parents were not home. I don't remember much up to the point of being in bed with him. Just that we went upstairs to a bedroom to make out and he wanted to just be naked with me. And for some reason I told him to be careful not to get me pregnant. Only because of what I had heard about possibly getting pregnant. He was shocked. I told him to be careful and he thought I meant that I wanted to have sex. So in that split second of a moment, I said okay. He was shocked and so we did.

I was kind of numb the whole time. I was taking a moment to focus on what was happening. Feeling that sensation of the pain of him entering me and breaking that thin skin. I was surprised at myself for doing it and knew there was no road back.

It didn't hurt a lot. I was so shocked that I was actually doing it that I was in a daze. I was stunned and hopeful that he would love me more. I think he had trouble getting it in at the very beginning. He was very sweet and awkward too. No eye contact. I remember that.

There was no best or worst for me. The whole thing was so unplanned and sudden. I was in shock. I remember afterwards, a girl peeked her head in the room as if she didn't know we were there. I thought, "Oh well everyone will know now." But I was such an insecure girl that I thought if people knew, it made me a bit cooler. I remember a strange moment when we went back downstairs to lie out in the sun. I looked down on my leg and right below my shorts, on my left leg, was a bit of blood. I quickly wiped it away and looked to see if anyone saw. I just remember that moment so well. I also remember looking in the mirror that night and thinking, "Do I look different?" Still just hoping that he loved me and wanted me more now.

I think I told a girlfriend or two. The hardest part was telling my next boyfriend. We had moved down south to another state. It was so painful to move away from Hank but was probably the best thing for me. Three months after I left, he got another girl pregnant. But my new boyfriend was such a wonderful, nice guy. We met at church. He was a virgin. And it was a bit tainted that I wasn't. He had a hard time with it.

Hank ended up marrying the girl that he got pregnant. They had five kids as far as I know. Just for fun recently, I looked him up online. He is in a band again. Looks great. But still in the same small town, with a bunch of kids to take care of.

I chose to lose my virginity at that time because I was just an insecure little girl. I loved him. Deep first love. At least it was with someone I loved. I just wish it was for the right reasons and planned.

This began a whole phase of my life where I thought that in order to be close with a man, you had to have sex with him. Also, it was a bit empowering to me to feel wanted, even if it wasn't for the right reasons. I now know that it is so much more empowering to be respected and to have sex as a mutually fun activity to share and grow with.

Hank and I didn't use any birth control because it was so unplanned. We hardly ever did after that and it is only by pure luck that I am not that girl with five kids.

Looking back, I do wish I had waited for a better relationship when I was a stronger young woman. Had it planned out better. I really wish that I'd had an open dialogue with my parents about it all. I know it would have helped me. Having sex that young just opened me to a world that I was not emotionally ready for. Of course at the time I thought I was. But I now see that it made me a sexual person too early. I think it is a huge responsibility and that, as women, we need to know the difference between being close to someone and having sex with them. Sex brings out insecurities, even when you are an adult. Once you add sex to a relationship, women expect more from the man and men are afraid that they are going to expect more. So when you wait for the right time, not just the fun time, it propels a relationship in the right direction. Gives you a new territory to explore. Instead of throwing it in too early and then the relationship is focused on the sex. Not much else. And there is so much more!

I *will never forget her placing her hand on my arm as she turned to go. I was stunned, frozen in time and heartbroken.*

Male: I am 52. I was 17.

The spring of 1971 was rushing into full bloom. The evenings were gradually becoming longer and the foliage colorful and thick. With the seasonal rebirth came that wonderful sense of excitement high school seniors experience as they finish their school duties and prepare to move onto the next phase of their lives. I was seventeen, finishing up varsity baseball and planning on attending college in the fall. I was also enjoying the introduction to the wonders of the female personality and body. You see, I was a late bloomer.

I had just dated for the first time. Her name was Kathy. A vivacious blue-eyed blonde with the nicest set of breasts one can imagine. We had gone through our flirting ritual until both had the nerve to actually agree to go see a movie on a Friday night. I picked her up at her house, met her parents and we were off. We met some friends at a local drive-in movie and sat outside our cars in chairs talking, laughing and otherwise being young. Kathy was our class flirt, so it was no surprise that she was busy with many. I, being a shy pleaser, enjoyed the moment chatting with others. As the night progressed, Kathy gravitated back towards me. Bolstered by a few cold beers, we held hands, laughed and exchanged a few quick kisses. Soon we decided to retreat to the back seat of my 1955 Chevrolet Belair. There we kissed. Kathy graciously allowed me fondle her breasts but stopped anything further. After some time, we stopped, got out of the car and rejoined the others in the group.

Back amongst the group, I was approached by Pam. She was the neighboring town's police chief's daughter and a year older than me. Tall with succulent lips, Pam moved with an air of confidence. We immediately hit it off, laughing, talking and otherwise completely comfortable around each other. Even Kathy, while making the social rounds, took notice. Things came to a head when I went to the restroom and was met near there by Kathy. The long and short of it was that Kathy encouraged me to pursue Pam. Kathy would ride home with a girlfriend. Strangely, we were both at peace and mature beyond our years in a situation like this. To this day I remain amazed with Kathy's grace.

Pam and I left the drive-in movie shortly thereafter. It was a gorgeous night, about 11:30 pm. We ate a banana split at a local diner and continued an extremely easy time together. We headed towards her hometown along a back road.

Along the way we sat close, holding hands, touching and enjoying a few kisses. I recall the tingles I felt as she placed her warm hand upon my bare bicep as we drove. Soon we pulled into the driveway of an old empty farm and stopped by the weathered barn, out of sight. We kissed passionately. Our hands freely flowed to parts of our bodies that brought instant joy. I had never felt such pleasure. Both of us were athletes in our prime with bodies to show for it. To this day the thought of Pam running her fingers over my stomach muscles causes erotic stirrings. Pam was quite comfortable with what we were doing. She explored every bit as much as I did. We held our kisses for what seemed to be an eternity while I ran my fingers through her thick, long dark hair.

I had little clue of what to do next. I had no rubber with me and I was quite concerned about getting her pregnant but could not stop. Unlike me, Pam was not a virgin. We fit wonderfully together and I did take the time to savor the first time. To this day there is no finer feeling.

After we were finished, we sat there for quite awhile and Pam again took the lead. She asked if I was okay, to which I answered more than she could know. I was at this time deathly afraid she would become pregnant and I told her so. She told me not to worry. But I did anyway.

I dropped her off at home around 1:15 am. Thankfully, her parents were asleep and she slipped into the house unnoticed. I had thoughts of venereal disease but quickly changed my thoughts to just how incredible it had been. While I knew who Pam was, we had never been friends or anything before.

As you can imagine, I instantly had the biggest crush on her. I lay awake that night in my bed wanting to call her. I wanted to see her again the next day. Well, I did get my wish.

There was a dance the next night at our high school. I had called Pam during the day to see if she wanted to go but got no call back. I attended the dance anxiously wanting to see her there. Unfortunately, she did not attend.

After the dance, I went to a drive-in to eat and hang out. To my surprise, Pam was there with a much older guy. I waved. She waved. Later in the evening, before they left, Pam told me what a wonderful time she had had the night before. However, she also said that she was committed to her college boyfriend but wished me the best. I will never forget her placing her hand on my arm as she turned to go. I was stunned, frozen in time and heartbroken. But also seemed to understand. I went over to be with my guy friends. We lit up a big fat cigar. Not long after, Pam left with her boyfriend. I finished my cigar and went home. I cried very hard.

After graduation, college would have to wait. I got my draft notice and joined the Navy Reserves. I worked in road construction. Pam went on to marry her boyfriend and have a family. Twenty-five years later I returned to speak at my high school homecoming. Several of us had dinner, including Pam and her husband. Not a word was spoken of our time together then or at any time previous.

Certainly, there have been no regrets. I consider myself so fortunate to have had my first sexual experience with someone as kind, giving and secure as Pam. It was incredible. I find myself at age fifty-two still having sex along the same lines and pace as that evening. I came away feeling that sex is a wonderful gift to experience with that special person.

*H*e was Winston and he sang baritone and played a mean concert violin and looked vaguely like Hollywood's idea of a Middle Eastern terrorist.

Female: I am 46 now. I was 21 then—nearly 22.

Did I have expectations of how I wanted it to be? Hmmmm...yeah. Big ones. That's why I waited until I was almost twenty-two. Partially I wanted to wait until I was with someone I genuinely cared about. But partially, I waited so long because when I was a teenager, I was hanging around with teenagers. The last thing I wanted was to lose my virginity to some know-nothing, clumsy, inexperienced kid who didn't know one end of a woman from another. I figured one of us should know what we were doing. So I guess you could say my expectations were fairly high.

He was Winston and he sang baritone and played a mean concert violin and looked vaguely like Hollywood's idea of a Middle Eastern terrorist. He had long, bushy hair he wore in a ponytail, was six feet two and weighed about two hundred forty pounds. He was huge and sexy and funny and brilliant and entirely emotionally unavailable. I fell in love at first sight. He barely noticed me until we'd met the fifth or sixth time. We began dating about three weeks after we'd met. We had sex for the first time about three dates in, if memory serves.

As for parental advice, my mom wasn't in my life—we'd been estranged for about five years at that point. Before that, growing up, my mom was very sexually liberal, talking openly and often about sex and contraception and telling me that, when I was ready, she'd be there to get me birth control pills or whatever I needed. I think she was a little disappointed I'd waited so long—she wanted to be the hip, cool mom that accompanied her daughter to Planned Parenthood. By the time I hooked up with Winston though, she was gone; I was fully capable of driving my own self to Planned Parenthood. My father's advice was limited to, "Don't get pregnant." So the Planned Parenthood thing dovetailed nicely.

I didn't get a whole lot of misinformation about sex as a youngster. It was probably due to my mother's unflagging forthrightness (to the point of obnoxiousness) when it came to the facts of sex. Also, I had an amazing human biology teacher when I was a sophomore in my Catholic high school who used her biology class to teach us the very detailed workings of the male and female reproductive systems. It should be noted that I went home with my hand-outs and textbooks and proceeded to correct a few of my mother's little erroneous ideas that she had about the menstrual cycle and ovulation. It's worth noting that, had I set my mother straight on this topic when she was a teenager, I might not be here today.

One fact from my circle of friends, which colored our view of sex and virginity, is that the first person in our group to lose her virginity lost it to date rape. It was something we'd never really considered until it happened to one of us. How could a boy we all knew, that we all trusted, that we'd smoked dope with and drank with, that we'd all kind of fantasized about, because, let's face it, he was hot—how could he betray not just her trust but all of our trust? Suddenly it wasn't just this boy, it was all boys and men. Because if one of your inner circle could steal something so precious—and from a girl he knew fairly well—then none of us were safe. Maybe that contributed to my waiting so long too. I had to feel I could trust someone enough to let him get that close.

Though I attended parochial schools from the time I was ten years old, religion had little impact on my sexual decisions. I figure if God hadn't meant for us to enjoy sex, he'd never have invented the orgasm. Pretty much end of story there.

It was in his bed—a twin, of all things—in his mother's house. It wasn't a surprise: It was plotted and planned from the beginning. I had started using the pill shortly before that and my second month didn't start until after we'd been dating for a week or so. As soon as I was certain I was fully protected, that was that. I was done with my virginity and it was done with me. (Ahhh the days before herpes and AIDS!).

I do recall something that I've forgotten over the years until I was thinking about writing this. He didn't know I was a virgin. I didn't tell him. I was almost twenty-two and I was afraid he'd think I was freak if he knew. Or he'd think I'd put too much weight in the act and he'd get spooked and run (which he did anyway). But that first time, he thought that I had very little (as opposed to no) experience.

I recall that I was very glad I waited. He was very sweet and kind. He really cared for me. I don't think I really valued that quite so much until that moment. The memory of the mechanics of it all escapes me at this point. It was a long time ago. It did hurt quite a bit at first but his consideration and his finesse (he was very experienced) was precious and reassuring. I can't really tell you what I was thinking, except that I wished I had told him that this was my first time. I didn't spend a lot of time preoccupied with that. I also remember thinking that I'd spent a lot of time doing a lot of other things when I could have been having sex. And that sex had the potential for being the best thing ever.

The best part was being that close to another person. The worst part was the pain. Afterward, I felt relieved. Relieved that the first time was past me, that I wasn't a virgin in my twenties anymore, that I didn't have to worry about when or who or where. My first time was actually quite pleasant, compared to some of my friends' stories: the date rape victim, my other friend whose boyfriend made love to her for the first time the night she was crowned prom queen, then dumped her three days later and on and on. I was just a girl in love with guy who loved her back—until he couldn't anymore and then he left. It left me knowing that sex was a good thing that added to a relationship when things were good but couldn't fix it when it went south. I'm still lousy at the whole "sports sex" thing but I'm not sure if that's because my first time was with someone I loved, or if I chose my first time with someone I loved because I couldn't stomach "sports sex." It's a mystery.

He and I still communicate via email from time to time. We have scads of mutual friends who fill me in on his life and (I have it on good authority) fill him in on mine. I remember my first time fondly and he set the bar really, really high in terms of prowess, affection and skill. I've only found one other person who could even come close to him in that regard and he trails a distant second. Of course, it hasn't exactly been the Cavalcade of Stars for me. You can count the number of men I've been with on the fingers of both hands (and still have a couple left over). I'm a long-term monogamy girl. I think this is just in my chemical make-up, rather than something I learned.

The only thing I'd change now is that I'd have told him I was a virgin. I think I sold him a little short on that one. And it would have been nice if we'd both shared the experience of my first time as such together. Perhaps it was my withholding the truth that ultimately led to his withdrawing his affection and backing away. Now I'll never know if that little white lie cost me dearly.

Advice for virgins? I can only tell you what I told my daughter when she was thirteen. Virginity isn't something you lose. It's not your house key or your favorite charcoal pencil or a dollar. You don't misplace it. It's something that's yours that only you can choose to give away. It's as precious or meaningless as you make it and I don't mean that in a pejorative way— only that each woman must put her own value on her first time. Sometimes it's something you just want to rid yourself of and sometimes it's a gift that you want to bestow on someone who means the world to you. Virginity is in your head, not between your legs. If you give it with a pure heart and an open spirit, if you protect yourself, physically and spiritually and if you're ready, then nothing bad can come of it.

?¿?¿?¿? Benjamin Franklin's Letter

*M*Y DEAR FRIEND:

I know of no Medicine fit to diminish the violent natural inclination you mention; and if I did, I think I should not communicate it to you. Marriage is the proper Remedy. It is the most natural State of Man and therefore the State in which you will find solid Happiness. Your Reason against entering into it at present appears to be not well founded. The Circumstantial Advantages you have in View by Postponing it, are not only uncertain but they are small in comparison with the Thing itself, the being married and settled. It is the Man and Woman united that makes the complete Being. Separate she wants his force of Body and Strength of Reason; he her Softness, Sensibility and acute Discernment. Together they are most likely to succeed in the World. A single Man has not nearly the Value he would have in that State of Union. He is an incomplete Animal. He resembles the odd Half of a Pair of Scissors.

If you get a prudent, healthy wife, your Industry in your Profession, with her good Economy, will be a Fortune sufficient.

But if you will not take this Counsel and persist in thinking that Commerce with the Sex is inevitable, then I repeat my former Advice that in your Amours you should prefer old Women to young ones. This you call a Paradox and demand my reasons. They are these:

1.   Because they have more Knowledge of the world and their Minds are better stored with Observations; their conversation is more improving and more lastingly agreeable.
2.   Because when Women cease to be handsome, they study to be good. To maintain their Influence over Man, they supply the Diminution of Beauty by an Augmentation of Utility. They learn to do a thousand Services, small and great and are the most tender and useful of Friends when you are sick. Thus they continue amiable. And hence there is hardly such a thing to be found as an Old Woman who is not a good Woman.
3.   Because there is no hazard of children, which irregularly produced may be attended with much inconvenience.
4.   Because through more Experience they are more prudent and discreet in conducting an Intrigue to prevent Suspicion. The Commerce with them is therefore safer with regard to your reputation; and regard to theirs, if the Affair should happen to be known, considerate People might be inclined to excuse an old Woman, who would kindly take care of a young Man, form

his manners by her good Councils and prevent his ruining his Health and Fortune among mercenary Prostitutes.

5.   Because in every Animal that walks upright, the Deficiency of the Fluids that fill the Muscles appears first in the highest Part. The Face first grows lank and Wrinkled; then the Neck; then the Breast and Arms; the lower parts continuing to the last as plump as ever; so that covering all above with a Basket and regarding only what is below the Girdle, it is impossible of two Women to know an old one from a young one. And as in the Dark all Cats are grey, the Pleasure of Corporal Enjoyment with an old Woman is at least equal and frequently superior; every Knack being by Practice capable by improvement.

6.   Because the sin is less. The Debauching of a Virgin may be her Ruin and make her Life unhappy.

7.   Because the Compunction is less. The having made a young Girl miserable may give you frequent bitter Reflections; none of which can attend making an old Woman happy.

8.   8th & lastly. They are so grateful!!!

Thus much for my Paradox. But still I advise you to marry immediately; being sincerely

Your Affectionate Friend,
Benj. Franklin

Kimberley Johnson and Ann Werner are a mother/daughter writing team and reside in Northern California.

Please visit us on the web: www.arkstories.com

Made in the USA
Lexington, KY
13 May 2014